The Magic of

LABYRINTHS

The Magic of

LABYRINTHS

Following Your Path, Finding Your Center

LIZ SIMPSON

Element
An Imprint of HarperCollins*Publishers*
77–85 Fulham Palace Road
Hammersmith, London W6 8JB

element™

Element is a trade mark of
HarperCollins*Publishers* Limited

First published 2002

10 9 8 7 6 5 4 3 2 1

A catalogue record for this book
is available from the British Library

ISBN 0 00 712047 8

Illustrations by Jeff Edwards

Printed and bound in Great Britain by
Scotprint, Haddington, East Lothian

CONTENTS

ACKNOWLEDGEMENTS

As a wise woman once remarked to me, the labyrinth is not about "me," it's about "us." The same is true of books. I could not have written this one without the generosity of spirit I received from so many inspiring individuals. Their support and the openness with which they shared their personal stories and wisdom have helped make the writing of this book an especially joyous experience for me. I would therefore like to extend my special thanks to:

Kim Anderson

Neil Anderson

Jim Buchanan

Dr. Alex Champion

Joan Champion

Kathy Doore

Robert Ferré

Lea Goode-Harris

Nicholas Halpin

Joyce Leake

Prof. Paula Lemmon

Sig Lonegren

Rae Ann Kumelos Mahon

Marge McCarthy

Julie Mitchell

Joseph Rafalo

Taylor Ray

Jeff Saward

Dr. Lynne A. Texter

Calvin Vanderhoof

Dale Vanderhoof

I would like to dedicate this book to my husband, Douglas Barnes. There is a saying I'm fond of: "A mind once stretched by a new idea never goes back to its original dimensions." No one has ever stretched me as much as you, Doug, for which I am ever grateful.

Labyrinth

*A walking meditation, a spiritual tool,
a means of coming to one's spiritual center.*

Viewed from exterior angles, a device that appears complicated and bewildering but, once experienced, is found to be a single pathway ("unicursal") that winds inextricably towards its center and requires you simply to take the same route out.

Maze

delirium, delusion, disappointment.

A network of interconnecting passages designed for trickery and deception. A complex puzzle that, without guidance, is difficult or impossible to navigate to a successful conclusion.

INTRODUCTION

Instead of searching for what you do not have,
Find out what it is you have never lost.

SRI NISARGADATTA MAHARAJ (1897–1981), FROM "I AM THAT"

What is a labyrinth? How does it differ from a maze? And why are so many people across the world today embracing a symbol that is thousands of years old? It is these, and other questions, that this book aims to address – but as a guidebook, rather than a set of rigid rules that have to be followed. Because what is so exciting about labyrinths is that they lend themselves to individual interpretation. There is no single labyrinth pattern, nor is there a right or wrong way to walk a labyrinth. Each experience is unique and, if welcomed, can offer valuable insights about how to navigate life and address its challenges.

The beauty of the labyrinth motif is that its appeal is so multi-faceted. As a metaphor for life's journey, the labyrinth prompts us to think about the way we choose to travel that path — whether we savor each moment, secure in the belief that while life's problems will continue to challenge us, we have the inner resources and confidence to solve them. Or whether we act like distracted on-lookers — always wondering why someone else seems to have the better deal. Consciously walking the labyrinth can cause you to reflect on whether life is something that just happens to you, or is an experience that you choose to truly engage with. The labyrinth symbol can help you re-appraise your goals in life — to stop looking for a "quick fix" by latching onto this guru or that and to accept full responsibility for your own spiritual enlightenment. After embracing the labyrinth as a metaphor for journeying into our deeper, hidden, authentic selves, many have been inspired to recognize that the source of contentment and wisdom lies within. Since walking the labyrinth — consciously and with respect — has prompted others to ask themselves questions like these, then it is likely to do the same for you. The labyrinth is not just a philosophical tool but lends itself to many practical applications. Here are a few of the ways in which labyrinth symbolism can be integrated into your life:

- *as a form of walking meditation, particularly for people who find it hard to sit still;*
- *to relax and release stress;*
- *to stimulate creative thinking and problem-solving;*
- *to assist in focusing on your breath;*
- *to work with your chakra system and the flow of chi;*
- *to get in touch with your inner or higher self;*

- *to connect with the Earth and more fully appreciate your environment;*
- *to create a stillness in which you can hear the whisper of your intuition;*
- *to do something nice for yourself — by yourself;*
- *to illustrate that you alone are responsible for the path you chart through life;*
- *to reconnect you to the Hero within.*

If you are challenged in any of these areas or if you are seeking a more grounded and balanced life, then there will undoubtedly be something within these pages that will arouse your interest and help you find new ways to approach these challenges and help you achieve your goals.

The Magic of Labyrinths is comparable to a journey. Like the labyrinth, while there is a commencement there is no definitive ending. That is entirely consistent with the nature of self-discovery. There are always more questions, more adventures and more lessons to participate in. We are spiritual students who, once committed to the journey, discover what it takes to be the most accomplished human graduates we can be. Within these pages you will be encouraged to re-examine your attitude to the challenging, complex and frequently perplexing pathway of life. A pathway that does not have to be a maze-like puzzle full of dead ends and frustrations, but a single route to an inevitable and glorious goal — self-mastery.

Indeed, of all the methods of self-understanding that I have introduced to friends, coaching clients and others, employing the labyrinth symbol — as a walking, finger or doodling meditation — has never failed to elicit powerful insights with which they have claimed a richly rewarding life. What specifically will you discover about labyrinths in this book and how you can apply them to your life? Here is a brief overview.

In Chapter One we will establish the historical contexts in which the labyrinth symbol emerged and was disseminated. Our journey takes us from stone-age Siberia, through Roman and Medieval times to the present day. We will travel through time from Egypt and Mauritania in Africa to picturesque villages in Britain and Scandinavia. You will read how the labyrinth symbol impacted Roman youths and Welsh shepherd boys, Native American tribes people and contemporary Latin scholars. And you will learn how pagan traditions were blended with the Christian Church's faith, explaining why so many labyrinths were established on the walls and floors of medieval cathedrals throughout France, Italy, and Britain.

Chapter Two looks more closely at how the various labyrinth patterns developed – the Classical Cretan motif, the medieval Christian and Roman mosaics, as well as new, contemporary versions. Once again, our journey together will take us across time and space to explore the labyrinths and other wheel-like symbols of Ireland, Peru, the United States, and Tibet, in addition to the palace of the legendary King Minos in Crete, the setting for the mythical tale of Theseus and the Minotaur. Our adventure will take in the significance of shape and numbers, place and energy. By which time you will have an appreciation of how the site of labyrinths is just as important as their size or design.

Throughout Chapter Three we journey inwards. By exploring the myth of Theseus and the Minotaur we determine the difference between a maze and a labyrinth and how we allow our minds to react to life as a diabolical puzzle or a direct, albeit circuitous, route to our goals. In particular, we will look at different ways in which the labyrinth experience can facilitate a paradigm shift in your approach to life, expanding on four themes which relate to the Hero's journey – The Call to Change, the Trial, Facing up to Doubt and Rebirth or "resurrection." You will find out how the Hero's journey is a common theme woven by storytellers from Homer to Hollywood and what it means to be a Hero in your own life.

Chapter Four examines the relevance of ritual and how engaging in regular practices can help you cope with change by reinforcing the message that change is never wholesale in one's life, but always comes alongside a degree of continuity. Here we will focus on one particular kind of ritual, the pilgrimage, and look at how walking the labyrinth offers the same kind of spiritual journey – one that is not tied to any religion and can be both an individual, personal experience as well as one to be shared by a community. In this chapter, you will also learn how to draw a Classical seven-circuit labyrinth and how to use that technique as a relaxation, chakra balancing, problem solving, and creative visualization tool.

Labyrinths will really come to life for you in Chapter Five where we explore not only how you might build a labyrinth for yourself, but also how community groups are embracing this symbol within schools, prisons, spas, community centers, hospitals, universities and as memorials to people and pets. By learning from the lessons arising from the stories offered in this chapter, you will discover how easy it can be for your community venture to create a labyrinth for relatively little money. Within each story you will read about the different materials you can use in the construction of your own labyrinth — whether temporary or permanent, canvas or computer generated — according to your specific needs, space, and budget.

Finally, in Chapter Six, you are presented with a collection of personal stories about labyrinths. These illustrate how a wide range of individuals — many of who have only recently been introduced to them — have benefited from occasional or regular exposure to labyrinths.

The labyrinth is an enigmatic symbol. It is both extraordinarily complex and extraordinarily simple. It can be used as a tool for individual introspection and as a catalyst for creating community spirit. After all, no hero ever has to tackle a journey completely alone. There are always friends and accomplices who will share in the challenges and dangers and who will be willing to discuss, analyze and help you face the fears associated with walking a new, more spiritually inspiring path.

The labyrinth, experienced interactively — that is, actually being *in it* — can seem a dark, frightening, and provocative place. It isn't really — as you will soon discover — that is just our perception of it. Before you decide whether you are up to venturing inside listen to the words of Nietzsche:

> *Believe me! The secret of reaping the greatest fruitfulness and the greatest enjoyment from life is to live dangerously.*

By picking up this book and reading thus far you are up to that challenge. Enjoy the journey!

chapter 1

THE HISTORY OF THE LABYRINTH

The shaman believes that the world of the human and the world of nature are essentially reflections of each other.

STANLEY KRIPPNER, "THE POWER OF PLACE"

*M*uch of what is out there about the history and development of labyrinths is more conjecture than fact. While we know a certain amount about the "what," "where," and "when," we can only come up with our own interpretations of the "who" and the "why." What follows is a potted history – a sort of labyrinth time-line that puts this into some sort of context.

There are any number of "firsts" attributed to the application of labyrinths around the globe. Jacques Attali writes that the oldest known graphic representation of a labyrinth is carved on a piece of mammoth ivory found in a Paleolithic tomb in Siberia (older than 5000 B.C.). Labyrinth historian, W.H. Matthews, refers to one of the seven Ancient Wonders of the World – the Egyptian labyrinth, tomb of Amenemhet III, as the earliest known labyrinth structure, built over 4,000 years ago. And British maze designer, Adrian Fisher, points to a rock carving of a seven-circuit labyrinth at Luzzanas in Sardinia as being possibly the world's oldest surviving labyrinth (c. 2500–2000B.C.).

The seven-circuit labyrinth at Luzzanas, Sardinia, may be the world's oldest surviving labyrinth.

Certainly, as Attali points out, the labyrinth symbol has been found on Neolithic figurines discovered near Belgrade in Yugoslavia, at the ruins of Kunlani near Madras in India and on a block of granite in the Wicklow Mountains in Ireland. Plus, one of the designs produced by the Yombas of Mauritania (an Islamic Republic between Senegal and Western Sahara, Africa) describes a giraffe alongside a labyrinth in which a bird is being mesmerized by a snake.

Regardless of where the labyrinth concept originated, this symbol has captured the imagination of cultures worldwide. Navigating their way through turf mazes – unicursal labyrinths cut into grass – was a popular game for Roman children. Indeed, many British examples still in existence have been found to have been sited close to Roman encampments and major Roman roads. This is the case at Alkborough, South Humberside, where there is a 44ft diameter turf labyrinth known as "Julian's Bower." One correspondent, writing in the mid-nineteenth century, recalls how he and his school friends would run in and out of the labyrinth as part of their May Day celebrations. While no one knows exactly when it was constructed, it is believed to have been built before 1671. However, there are many turf labyrinths throughout Britain that predate that. At Boughton Green in Northamptonshire there was one known as the "Shepherd's Ring" or "Shepherd's Race" whose "treading" was a key feature of the village's June fair – an event dating back to the middle of the fourteenth century. This tradition of cutting a labyrinth pattern into hillsides also became a common custom of Welsh shepherd boys who tended their flocks alone on the mountains and may have offered them some light relief from a tedious occupation. Among the general population in earlier times, these turf mazes were often given the epithet "Troy Towns."

Troy Towns

Various suggestions have been put forward as to why labyrinths were called "Troy Towns" or "Walls of Troy" in Britain, "Caerdroia" in Wales and "Trojeborn" in Scandinavia. According to a fifteenth century French manuscript detailing a gentleman's journey to Jerusalem, now in the British Museum, the Knossos labyrinth with which we associate the Minotaur legend was at that time commonly known as "The City of Troy." According to the poet Virgil (70 B.C.–19 A.D.), writing about the Trojan Wars (c. 1,300–1,200 B.C.), the only Trojan prince to escape after the fall of Troy was Aeneas, who fled to Italy with his father and son. This young boy is said to have popularized a processional parade or dance that wealthy Roman youths subsequently re-enacted, which was known as the "Game of Troy." (Aeneas is said to have founded Lavinium, from where the founders of Rome originated.) This youthful reconstruction of the epic conflict has also been found depicted on an Etruscan vase found at Tragliatella which is decorated with figures engaging in the Lusus Trojae *or "Game of Troy," alongside a Classical seven-circuit labyrinth.*

Legend has it that Aeneas' great-grandson, Brutus was sent into exile and, after freeing the descendants of Trojan captives, founded a new kingdom which was named after him – Britain. This may account for the fact that while turf mazes, many still surviving, exist in other parts of Europe, the greatest proliferation of them is in Britain.

Given the fact that so many of these stories were handed down by word of mouth for centuries, the "Game of Troy" may have become mixed up with the Crane Dance said to have originated with Theseus and his party after escaping from the Knossos maze (see page 69).

Later, the Roman Catholic Church embraced the labyrinth motif, describing it on the floors of churches and cathedrals during the thirteenth century, principally across Italy and France. The most famous examples can still be seen at Chartres and Amiens, although many have subsequently been destroyed – including those at Rheims, Sens, and Auxerre Cathedrals.

Despite having in common a single pathway leading to and from the center, there are considerable variations on the general theme. Not all church labyrinths are circular. Some are octagonal, like the example at Amiens. Others have additional corner pieces (called "bastions" or "bellows"), as with the Rheims example. A very early labyrinth, dating back to the fourth century in the Church of Reparatus in Orleansville, Algeria, is square. Not all churches favored pavement labyrinths either. The entrance walls of many Italian churches, like that of Lucca Cathedral (*see* page 36), were inscribed with small finger labyrinths that worshipers could trace before entering.

Across the Atlantic, the Hopi Indians of Arizona had their own version of the labyrinth symbol, known as the "Man in the Maze," which continues to be inscribed on jewelry and other artifacts to this day. Unlike the European labyrinth designs, the Hopi example features the entrance at the top rather than the bottom, and there is always a male figure portrayed at the mouth. This is reminiscent of the games played by young men in Scandinavia who would challenge each other at the entrance to the labyrinth to see who could be the first to reach the female waiting for them in the center.

From several millennia B.C. through to the present time, there have been examples of the labyrinth found in the Far East, Scandinavia, the Americas, and throughout Europe. In the sixteenth century, multicursal hedge mazes became popular as formal gardens began to be established in Europe and wealthy patrons looked to be amused and challenged by these puzzles. Many examples can be found in France, including the hedge maze built at the Palace of Versailles for Louis XIV. The one that was created at the palace of Het Loo in Holland became the inspiration for the maze established in 1690 at Hampton Court, Henry VIII's palace south-west of London. Given the complexity of their construction and the cost of their upkeep, hedge mazes are mainly found near castles, within the gardens of large country houses and, more recently, in public gardens and large parks.

However fascinating puzzle mazes have been over the past four hundred years, the unicursal labyrinth is now enjoying a renaissance – particularly thanks to the leadership given by Dr. Lauren Artress of Grace Cathedral in San Francisco, California where there is both an outdoor terrazzo labyrinth and an indoor tapestry one. As you will discover from the personal stories in this book, anyone with the desire to benefit from this calming, meditative and – some say – healing tool, can produce a labyrinth for themselves, irrespective of space, materials, or money.

ORIGINS OF THE LABYRINTH

So, we have no shortage of historical antecedents for the labyrinth motif, but where might it have originated, and who was responsible?

Established in 1690, the Hampton Court maze is probably the most impressive hedge maze in Britain.

Collective Unconscious

The most popular suggestion focuses on what the Swiss psychoanalyst, Carl Gustav Jung termed "the collective unconscious" – a universal thought that is captured and expressed simultaneously by groups separated by space and time. You have probably experienced this for yourself, when hitting upon a "unique" idea, only to find that someone else has been developing something almost identical at the same time.

The most common explanation for the proliferation of labyrinths across so many different cultures is that we are each responsive to subliminal perceptions. Jung argued that the collective unconscious is formed of two parts – instincts and archetypes, which are universally inherited and mutually dependant. While our instincts are biological – such as the flight, freeze or fight responses experienced when facing danger – the archetypes we each store in our unconscious memory are equally primordial but are higher, spiritually-charged functions.

The word "archetype" comes from the Greek *arch* meaning "origin" and *tupos* meaning "imprint." These universally understood themes or emotional models become significant to different people at different times in their lives – particularly during the periods we call "rites of passage." They are personified as characters we are all familiar with. Many of them feature prominently in fairy stories, such as the Wicked Stepmother, the Fairy Godmother, the Trickster, the Mentor, and the Shapeshifter. Certain key archetypes are specifically linked to the labyrinth as a symbol of our journey towards spiritual development. The most significant is the Hero – the role we take on when we pluck up the courage to embark on the quest to "find ourselves" and integrate all the fragmented pieces of the Self into one complete and balanced whole. (For more on this, *see* chapter 3.)

Then there is the Shadow archetype – the dark, suppressed, rejected energy which is depicted in stories as a monster, housed inside a dark cavern, which the Hero must confront and tame or vanquish in order to prevent his or her destruction. In our own lives, the Shadow represents all those parts of ourselves which we prefer not to acknowledge but most readily see and criticize in others. One of the most famous stories about a labyrinth is the myth of Theseus and the Minotaur where our hero enters the sinister maze-world of the beast in order to end the killing spree it engages in every nine years when fourteen young Athenian youths and maidens are sent to Crete as tribute to King Minos (*see* page 68).

Archetypes and myths – the stories woven around such universal models of human psychological development – were, in Jung's view, essential to our human need for self-understanding, as well as to help to mitigate our fear of personal isolation. Jung argued the concept of an inherited "Group Mind" or collective unconscious by demonstrating the similarity of mythologies across cultures, suggesting that these were the building blocks of religion.

Jung's fascination with the primordial imprinting that leads us to seek a spiritual or religious explanation for the world around us, and our role within it, was expressed through his drawings. It is said that every morning he would sketch small circles as representations of his inner state that day. Jung noticed how these circles, such as the mandalas used as meditation tools by eastern mystics – as with labyrinths – brought everything to a single central point. The great psychoanalyst's interpretation of this universal motif was that it symbolized the Self's incessant journey towards higher meaning and purpose.

Likewise, the labyrinth is a universally imprinted archetype or theme illustrating our life's journey towards spiritual development and completion. As you will discover later in this book, it can be used as both a personal tool and one that unites communities, thus fuelling our sense of Oneness with our environment.

One Mind, Many Applications?

There is a complementary view that also bears mentioning. One that may also explain the mysterious origins of the labyrinth and that similarly speaks to our psychological need to feel part of a whole. This alternative view helps to demonstrate that we are not so different from peoples who lived on this Earth 10, 20, 30 or even 40,000 years ago. Indeed, contemplating the enduring facets of human nature helps to reinforce the relevance of the labyrinth as an archetypal symbol that is as psychologically valuable to us today as it was way back when.

Much of our popular historical knowledge cloaks the fact that considerably more early cross-cultural contact took place than was once thought. For example, most children are taught that Henry the Navigator or Christopher Columbus "discovered" America in the fifteenth century.

Some may even have heard of Amerigo Vespucci or John Cabot (Giovanni Caboto) who, controversially, claimed to have preceded them. This completely disregards evidence that expeditions to the New World had been undertaken by peoples originally from Siberia (c. 70,000–9,000B.C.). Other suggested early explorers of the Americas, with varying degrees of evidence, range from Indonesians (c. 6,000–1,500B.C.), the Japanese (c. 5000B.C.) and Afro-Phoenicians (c. 1000B.C.–300A.D.).

Certainly, some archaeologists and historians now believe that the Vikings may have traveled down from Newfoundland to New England and even reached North Carolina. And it seems likely that these expeditions were not all one way, given the record of two Indians having been shipwrecked in Holland around 60B.C., causing considerable interest and excitement at the time. There are many other examples that provide a richer view of history than most of us were taught at school.

Given that there was considerable cross-cultural contact between peoples much earlier than we have been led to believe, this can be linked with contemporary evidence for the way ideas originating within one small group can spread like wildfire. Hence, we can see how a symbol such as the labyrinth could have come to enjoy such universal popularity from a single source.

Today we call it "viral marketing" or "buzz," but basically it is old-fashioned word of mouth. In his book *The Tipping Point*, Malcolm Gladwell outlines three criteria or rules for the proliferation of social epidemics and he discusses how certain messages, behaviors, ideas, and their products spread like infectious diseases. The concept of a labyrinth, stemming from a single source, meets all three of these criteria.

First, you need a small number of people with both the creativity to understand the impact of a new idea and the personal magnetism or charisma with which to promote it. Such people in early times were called "shamans." Shamanism, said to be the world's oldest religion, spiritual discipline and medical approach, originated in Siberia – and it was here that a labyrinth carving was found, dating back over 7,000 years. The shaman worldview offers an experiential path to knowledge, gained through the process of ritual, meditation and a concept of trials or tests that is akin to the Hero's journey through the labyrinth (*see* chapter 3). Like the labyrinth, while variations exist between cultures, the concept of shamanism is very similar whether in the Americas, Africa, and Australasia or Lapland, Malaysia, and Peru.

The shaman's role within a society was to straddle the world of reality and the world of spirit. As such they demonstrated that all-important psychological need which is now being explored more actively through environmental and spiritual groups – that of the interdependence and unity of nature and humankind. Interestingly, the shaman did not simply represent the Divine, as priests and other religious figures do. The shaman is Divine, in the way that we have been urged to think of ourselves by many prophets and philosophers, such as the fourteenth-century Christian mystic, Meister Eckhart, who said:

Here, in my own soul, the greatest of all miracles has taken place.
God has returned to God.

In the same way that the simple act of walking or tracing a labyrinth can unite body and spirit, the shaman demonstrated the spiritual affinity between plant, person, and place.

Malcolm Gladwell's second criterion explaining why certain concepts can spread rapidly across societies is that of "stickiness." By this he means the extent to which a message is memorable and impactful. Since Jung, together with Eastern mystics before him, have presented the image of life as a journey with a single pathway leading in to the center, it is not surprising that the labyrinth motif would have appealed to anyone who came into contact with it.

Given the potential of the labyrinth as a way of explaining the world and how we should best act on it, it can be imagined that one or a number of Siberian shamans found that this particular tool – a portable "mental map," simple to construct and easy to explain – helped them disseminate their worldview to other cultures. This may have happened in the same way that the "peace symbol," the original concept of one man, spread from being used in materials and on marches by the UK's Campaign for Nuclear Disarmament, to being a worldwide icon of peace. Being simple to produce and an image that resonated with billions of people around the globe, the peace symbol – like, possibly, the labyrinth – was one person's idea that "stuck." It was a local idea that fast became a global phenomenon.

The third criterion is "the power of context." Here again, we can relate back to Jung's hypothesis for the universal power of archetype and myth. The notion of something so simple yet complex as a labyrinth is as compelling to us in the twenty-first century as it was to our earliest ancestors. There is no reason to suggest that they would not have been concerned with the same big, philosophical questions that we still grapple with today – Why are we here? What is the purpose of our lives? What happens when we die? Like us, they would have wanted to better understand life and the purpose of it – and, in particular, how to feel happier and more fulfilled on this lifelong journey.

The psychologist, Abraham Maslow, formulated a hierarchy of needs in which security issues (such as the provision of shelter and food) are at the base of the triangle, with self-actualization (spiritual needs) at the pinnacle. However, this seems to over-simplify the human experience and before Maslow died he admitted that he might have got this the wrong way around. Just because prehistoric people had more pressing security concerns than most of us in the West today, that does not mean that they did not also seek deeper meaning and purpose in their lives.

The manner in which our ancestors explored these issues was through myths and there is considerable similarity in these stories, regardless of the culture. Indeed, rather than accepting that religious writers accessed the power of the collective unconscious, it may be that they borrowed and modified much earlier stories for which the power of context was universal. For instance, there is considerable similarity between archetypes appearing in the Assyro-Babylonian poem the Epic of Gilgamesh (c. 700B.C.) and the Old Testament of the Bible. Both feature a serpent, a woman who robs a hero of his innocence, and someone who survives a Great Flood.

LABYRINTHS AND MYTH

The labyrinth has long been associated with myths and legends, the most direct link being with the story of Theseus and the Minotaur (*see* page 66). But why should we be interested in centuries-old accounts of the exploits of fictional gods, goddesses and heroes? More particularly, why would they hold any relevance to us today?

Mythology is populated by archetypal characters who illustrate universal dispositions with which each one of us can relate at various times in our lives. Despite the culture or period in which these mythological tales were written, each one of us recognizes in them universal values around being and behaving. Within an oral tradition, myths ensured the values of a culture were broadcast from generation to generation. They also helped explain fundamental but complex philosophical issues in a way that was more palatable and easily understood – through stories about the adventures and lives of gods and heroes.

For example, no concept intrigues, terrifies, and holds us in awe more than death. Death has been the subject of introspection and debate since the earliest times when bodies, whether of Egyptian pharaohs or Neanderthal nomads, were buried with everything they might need for their next journey, into the "land beyond." We are fascinated by death from an early age when we ask, unsuccessfully, for confirmation of exactly what happens to us. I remember an occasion when we buried a goldfish in the back garden and my small son pressed me to tell him where it would go. Thinking I was being suitably spiritual in my instruction, I assured Graeme that the goldfish would go to heaven to be with God, only to find my son digging up the area the next day to check whether the fish had got there yet.

The labyrinth is typically associated with dark caves, the inner workings of our subconscious and the way in which we must constantly review our attitudes and behaviors so that we "kill off" any that are no longer useful to us in order to resurrect or discover ones that are. Not surprisingly, the labyrinth motif has been woven into a number of myths concerning death. Such myths also elaborate on the key role of women in the human experience. For example, Joseph Campbell relates the myth of the Malekula islanders in Vanuatu (formerly the New Hebrides) in the South Pacific who learn that their approach to the Land of the Dead will be halted by a female guardian. She draws a labyrinth design in the earth, then erases half of it and the soul's task is to complete the design perfectly before they will be allowed to pass through to the underworld. If they do not, then they will be eaten by her.

Unlike mazes with their dead ends, labyrinths are reminiscent of coiled snakes. According to the Hindu tradition, Kundalini is the serpent goddess who awakens whenever an individual embarks upon a spiritual journey. As they proceed on their path, overcoming challenges in the way of the hero, Kundalini journeys upwards, piercing each chakra in turn until, reaching the crown chakra, the subject is said to have achieved spiritual enlightenment. (For more on this, *see* page 75.)

Snake-like Imprints

Then there is a tale that comes from Arnhem Land in Australia's Northern Territory which is the aboriginal equivalent of the Biblical story of Noah's flood – only, as in many non-Christian examples, the story involves female protagonists, not a male one. Two sisters, one already a mother and the other pregnant, are forced to leave their home and begin to journey north. As they travel they give names to everything they see, bringing the stone animals, plants and insects to life. These women belonging to the Wagilag clan, camp alongside the Mirarrmina watering hole, unaware that it is the sacred home of the Giant Python, Wititj.

Angry at being disturbed, Wititj sucks up all the water and spits it out to form monsoon clouds that break and flood the land. The sisters begin to perform songs and dances in order to divert the waters. But the serpent swallows them and their offspring whole, raising himself into the sky to escape the deluge. In the heavens, he is admonished by his ancestors and they tell Wititj that he should not have swallowed all members of the same family. The great snake becomes ill and crashes to the ground, leaving a labyrinthine imprint in the earth, whereupon he spits out the women and children. Wagilag men who have followed them, learn of the songs and dance rituals performed by the women to halt the flooding and these are enacted during the monsoon season to ensure the continuation of nature's cycles.

In Arnhem Land, the giant python Wititj was said to be responsible for the cycle of the seasons.

Goddess Worship

The links between the labyrinth symbol and goddess worship – the means through which early people expressed their love and respect for Mother Earth – are strong. The meander pattern (*see* page 28), from which the Classical seven-circuit labyrinth may be derived, has been found on bird goddess figurines dating back to c. 18000–15000B.C. by Lake Baical in the Ukraine. Additionally, rituals engaged in across Scandinavia (where the largest concentration of labyrinths from antiquity can be found) involved males competing with each other to see who can reach the female in the center first. These games, conducted most frequently in eleven-circuit labyrinths, were very different from the formulaic rituals of the seven-circuit Troy Towns. Indeed, there is a suggested link between the number 7 and male energy and the connection between the number 11 and female energy (*see* page 35).

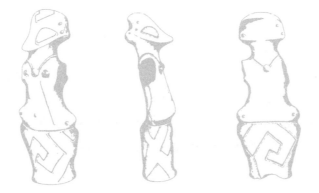

Bird goddess figurines from the Ukraine showing characteristic meander patterns.

Within the eleven-circuit stone labyrinths that proliferate throughout Finland and Sweden the goal of negotiating the labyrinth involved rescuing a young woman at the center. At Kopmanholm, to the north-east of Stockholm in Sweden, there is a stone labyrinth known as the *Jungfruringen* or "Virgin's Ring." This particular design has two entrances, one going in from the left, the other from the right. The game involved two young men racing to the center to see which one of them would reach the maiden first. A number of suggestions have been made as to what this game signifies. One is that the female in the center represents Helen, the acclaimed beauty over whom the Greeks and Trojans went to war. Another is that "saving the girl" is a metaphor for young men reclaiming their female energy in order to become whole human beings again. This pagan symbolism has also been found on a wall of a fifteenth-century church in Nyland, Finland where a painting of a labyrinth depicts a virgin waiting at the center.

Labyrinths in Popular Culture

In fairy stories, while labyrinths or mazes are seldom implicitly mentioned, the notion of the Prince hacking his way through a dense, complex forest in order to reach the Sleeping Beauty, is just one metaphor for the trials and tests one must engage in to reach a prized goal. Indeed, many such stories involve the protagonists enduring a series of tasks – for which they appear initially unprepared – that suggest a journey to find their female side (the "princess") in order to become complete human beings.

The Jungfruringen *or* Virgin's Ring, Sweden, *with its two entrances. Young men would race each other to reach the maiden in the center first.*

Given the richness and complexity of the labyrinth as a metaphor for life, this motif has captured the imagination of writers, most of who allude to intricacies or entanglements of one sort of another. In *Troilus and Cressida,* Shakespeare writes: "How now Thersites? What, lost in the Labyrinth of thy furie?" The poet Shelley opined: "From slavery and religion's labyrinth caves, Guide us." And from W.B. Yeats: "Does the imagination dwell the most, Upon a woman won or woman lost? If on the lost, admit you turned aside, From a great labyrinth out of pride."

In the world of popular fiction, labyrinths – explicit or allegorical – appear in the likes of Mervyn Peak's Gormenghast novel *Titus Groan*, in the description of the Stone Lanes region; as the Mines of Moria in J.R.R. Tolkien's *The Lord of the Rings* and in Terry Pratchett's *Small Gods* with the "booby-trapped labyrinth of Ephebe." J.K. Rowling has even incorporated a maze in the Tri-Wizard Tournament, that her hero must navigate at the end of *Harry Potter and the Goblet of Fire*.

But my favorite example of a labyrinth in a book is in Neil Gaiman's *Neverwhere*, described as a dark, contemporary *Alice in Wonderland*. In the story, an ordinary man named Richard Mayhew becomes trapped in London Below and must negotiate the labyrinth and its beast in order to reach and vanquish the ultimate enemy – an angel who has "gone bad." Mayhew alone succeeds where others (traditionally more powerful) in his party fail, despite losing the talisman that he had been told would ensure his safe passage through the labyrinth. After successfully killing the beast, our hero is told to apply its blood to his eyes and tongue so that he can negotiate the passages with ease.

The wonderful message of this part of the book is that facing and disposing of the "monster within" – a concept Jung referred to as our "shadow" – is a *precursor* to converting the journey from a puzzling maze into a labyrinth. By doing this, your way becomes "straight and true" during which you know "… instinctively every twist, every path, every alley …" Thus, Gaiman reminds us, tackling the inner Beast – whether that be our fears, our self-neglect, our cowardice or denial of reality – allows us to navigate life's journey by tapping into our inner compass or intuition. In this way we discover that life's path involves an easier and more straightforward approach than we originally thought. (For more on how we can change our own lives from resembling mazes to becoming more like labyrinths, *see* page 75.)

Also worth mentioning in this context is the movie *Labyrinth*, Jim Henson's dark, allegorical tale of a teenager who wishes her annoying baby brother would be taken away by goblins – and he is; a classic case of "beware of what you wish for." Our heroine, Sarah, is then given thirteen hours to rescue the boy, before he is turned into a goblin. She accomplishes her quest, which superficially involves solving riddles and a race against time, but in essence it concerns the process of growing up and discovering what is really important in life.

Labyrinths and Christianity

It may seem surprising that a symbol so obviously associated with pagan beliefs came to find its way into so many Christian churches. However, the taking over of pagan symbols and ideas was something the Roman Catholic Church engaged in extensively. For example, pagan communities tended to celebrate festivals every six to eight weeks, to mark the changing seasons and solar cycles. Because these were so well established throughout northern Europe, particularly in Britain, many were simply overlain with Christian symbolism. Hence, Yule or the winter solstice became Christmas, Samhain became All Saint's Day, and the spring equinox became Easter. The latter festival, incidentally, is named after the German fertility goddess Eostre or Ostara, which comes from the same root as the female hormone oestrogen. Not surprisingly, given the fertility link and the nature of female reproduction, the symbol of Eostre is an egg – hence the notion of Easter eggs, which was a custom engaged in by pagan communities long before Christianity came on the scene.

Indeed, it has been argued that the Christian figure of Mary, mother of Jesus Christ was recreated from the ancient concept of the Great Mother Goddess in her triple archetypal roles of Virgin, Mother, and Wise Woman. There were certainly plenty of precedents for virgin births among the pre-Christian pantheon of Gods. The oldest of divinities, Gaia, appeared out of nothing to give birth to Uranus, the starlit sky, while the patriarch of the Greek gods was originally called Zeus Marnas or "Virgin born Zeus." Any number of Greek heroes, including Perseus who slayed the Gorgon Medusa, and Jason of Argonaut fame, were said to be virgin born. The reason why the Christian church has resisted the worship of Mary as anything other than the earthly mother of Jesus was because she was based on a composite of many pagan goddesses. However, by giving this archetype a role to play within its religion, the Catholic Church ensured that their new, monotheist, patriarchal religion became relevant to people who were polytheist and largely matrifocal. As well as re-defining the Mother Goddess as the Virgin Mary, the Church changed many other pagan deities into saints. In one example, the Celtic goddess Brighid became St. Brigit (or Brigid).

In the same way that the Holy Roman Church appropriated existing pagan archetypes and festivals, it built its places of worship on sites which ancient peoples had long revered for their sacred energy. Many churches in England were built on "ley lines" (the phenomenon of electromagnetic energy sometimes called Earth "chi") because the only way the Catholic church could integrate non-Christians into their own religion was to appropriate the sacred sites at which they already worshipped.

The labyrinth is a wonderful tool that engages people easily and that can be used to address deeper issues around spirituality and the best way to journey through life. So, instead of throwing the baby out with the bathwater, the Christian Church appropriated it for its own needs. The Christian church could not change people's long-held faith, so they simply Christianized it. In the process, to set theirs apart from pagan examples, church labyrinths became more intricate in their design and ornate in their execution. They also became associated with Biblical cities, such as Jerusalem and Jericho – the latter possibly deriving from the Roman view of labyrinths as a kind of fortified city.

Contemporary Labyrinths

Aside from all the wonderful examples of labyrinths springing up around the world today – many of which we will read about in later chapters – this ancient symbol is proliferating on that most modern of tools – the Internet. If you are interested in the use of the labyrinth as a device in on-line and other interactive games, the World Wide Web will lead you, labyrinth-like, to the key resources.

One particularly inspiring use of the labyrinth on the computer is the on-line Lenten labyrinth. Professor Paula Lemmon teaches beginner's Latin classes at the Southwestern Methodist University in Dallas, Texas. For the last two years (at the time of writing), her department has created an on-line Lenten labyrinth for which the students are charged with providing translations (from Latin into English) of various classical and religious texts. The 2001 project is totally inter-active, with twelve candles pointing the way through this ancient devotional tool in order to illu-minate the images and words contained within. Traditionally linked to the concept of pilgrimage by the Christian church (*see also* page 94), the Lenten labyrinth allows the Web pilgrim to scroll through the Chartres design to read excerpts from medieval Latin texts (including Ovid's *Fasti*), accompanied by images of the Holy Land that were created by the nineteenth-century painter, David Roberts in 1842. These images come from the archives of the University's Bridwell Library, which holds a world-renowned collection of classical theological and other texts. This is the first time that images from David Roberts' Holy Land folio have been digitally distributed, and presents a rare opportunity to see his work (*see* Resources, page 174).

chapter 2

LABYRINTHINE PATTERNS

"… *everything an Indian does is in a circle, and that is because the Power of the World always works in circles, and everything tries to be round* …"

BLACK ELK, OGLALA LAKOTA, 1930

THE DEVELOPMENT OF THE LABYRINTH PATTERN

It may seem odd that if someone wanted to come up with a simple design symbolizing our journey through life, they did not just draw a straight line from A (birth) to (death). But then, is life ever that straightforward? The labyrinth motif has maintained its appeal because it speaks to the reality of having to navigate many twists and turns as we journey towards our goals.

However, while all labyrinths follow a general design comprising of a unicursal path, there are many variations on that theme, and it is these designs that we focus on in this chapter.

The Classical, Seven-circuit Pattern

The oldest labyrinth pattern is that of the Cretan labyrinth, so-named because of its association with that island civilization and religion. It comprises, typically, of seven concentric circuits, although this form exists from three circuits up to nineteen. The oldest British example to which a date can be ascribed is that of a carving on granite named the Hollywood Stone, now on display in the Museum of Antiquities in Dublin. The stone and its seven-circuit Cretan design was found on a pilgrim's track that wove its way through the Wicklow Mountains in Ireland from Hollywood to the Celtic monastic settlement at Glendalough.

When playing around with the labyrinth design, Jeff Saward the British editor of the labyrinth journal *Caerdroia* (*see* story on page 161, and Resources), together with a friend, worked out that the Classical seven-circuit labyrinth

The meander or "Greek Key" pattern is thought to be the basis of the Classical seven-circuit labyrinth design.

The Hollywood Stone, found on a pilgrim's way in the Wicklow Mountains, Ireland.

was simply a variation on a theme commonly depicted on Greek and Roman pottery – the meander. This meander pattern or "Greek key" was common to Old Europe many thousands of years before the Greek civilization flourished and indeed examples have been discovered on "Bird Goddess" figurines at Mezin in the Ukraine that date back to c. 18000–15000B.C.

While not resembling a labyrinth at first glance, when you twist this unbroken design into a circle it does indeed become labyrinth-like. The similarity is even more apparent when you look at the Man in the Maze motif of the Hopi tribe of Arizona, where the corners of that labyrinth are squared-off rather than curved. One modern example of this design – having the wider entrance and squared-off rather than curved corners – can be found outside the Museum of International Folk Art in Santa Fe, New Mexico (*see* story, page 121).

Interest in the meander design has been maintained over the centuries and, given the vast number of products available on the Internet that incorporate it, particularly jewelry and home furnishings, the interest continues unabated. One interior design company specializing in the Greek key design claims that introducing this pattern into the home helps achieve a sense of a bigger, warmer, softer, calmer, friendlier environment. Is this just marketing rhetoric or is there something special about the energy created by the meander pattern, as is claimed for the labyrinth? Certainly, earlier civilizations, such as that of the Greeks, stressed the importance of design for achieving harmonious living. They called this approach "sacred geometry" (*see* page 55).

The Man in the Maze motif from the Hopi tribe, Arizona. The squared-off corners are reminiscent of the "Greek Key" design.

Although it is the most common form, the classical Cretan labyrinth pattern does not have to comprise of seven circuits. One of the most unusual three-circuit labyrinths is featured high in the Peruvian Andes where ancient artists created gigantic geometric forms and animal outlines that are discernible only by air. These are the Nazca lines, named after the culture that flourished in the region during the sixth or seventh centuries. Thought variously to be the landing strips for alien spacecraft or to have astronomical/astrological importance, the Nazca images were formed by scraping away the top layer of the pampa to expose the chalky white gypsum underneath. These strange labyrinthine-like totems include that of the curling tail of a Monkey and the winding pathway formed by the outline of a Spider.

The Monkey and the Spider – two of the many ancient labyrinthine totems at Nazca, Peru.

Examples of Cretan labyrinths are manifold – from the plains of Peru to the basketry of the Native American tribes of Arizona. They appear as "turf mazes" throughout Britain and as stone labyrinths across Scandinavia. But this design, while the oldest, is not the only labyrinth pattern.

The Chartres, Eleven-circuit Pattern

The second labyrinth pattern is the medieval Christian or Chartres design which sprung up in Gothic cathedrals and churches – principally in France and Italy – during the twelfth century, although it may have been designed as early as the eighth century. However, ecclesiastical links between these pavement labyrinths and churches goes back much further. W.H. Matthews, who has conducted an exhaustive study of the history of mazes and labyrinths, reports that the oldest known example of a pavement labyrinth can be found in the Church of Reparatus in Orleansville, Algeria which is believed to date from the fourth century. This miniature example (just 8ft in diameter) comprises four quadrants like the Chartres design. It is very "meander like," having squared-off pathways rather than curved ones. In the center of this example there is a form of word puzzle on the letters that make up the words "Sancta Eclesia."

The number 7 – the number of pathways within the Classical Cretan labyrinth – occurs in many esoteric and religious groupings. For example, there are seven main chakras; the Mystery School at Chartres studied the Seven Liberal Arts – Arithmetica, Astronomica, Dialectica, Geometrica, Grammatica, Musica, and Rhetorica; and, according to the Old Testament (Genesis 2:3), when God completed his creation of the Earth and its inhabitants He blessed and sanctified the seventh

This labyrinth, in the Church of Reparatus in Orleansville, Algeria, dating from the fourth century, is the oldest known example of a pavement labyrinth. The letters in the center are a puzzle based on the words "Santa Eclesia."

day. Indeed, the Bible is full of references to the number 7, from the length of the Feast of Unleavened Bread (Exodus 12:19) to the seven sayings of Jesus uttered from the Cross.

So, given the widespread connection between the Christian religion and the number 7, why does the Chartres design consist of eleven rather than seven circuits? To answer this, we need to take a brief journey into the realm of numerology and sacred geometry.

Douglas Adams, author of *The Hitchhiker's Guide to the Galaxy* was not just being facetious when he wrote that the meaning of life was 42. Numerology – the study of numbers and their relationships – is an ancient occult or esoteric art. While it is believed to have originated with the Greek mathematician, Pythagoras, some experts argue that he learned about the prophetic nature of numbers from the Kabala. This early Hebrew work mainly consists of mystical practices aimed at uncovering the nature of divinity, creation, the soul and the earthly role of human beings. You may have had a small taste of numerology yourself when adding up the numeric relationship with the letters making up your name or your birth date. According to modern numerologists, such calculations offer clues to a person's talents, life challenges, basic values and the way they might best express themselves through their choice of work. Pythagoras is said to have developed a letter wheel by which he could predict – like an astrologer – the future events in a person's life based on their name.

Within numerology there are nine basic numbers (1–9), each with its own meanings, plus two "master" numbers – 11 and 22. While the number 7 is ascribed the characteristics of spirituality and mystery through analysis, awareness, meditation, and a cerebral (typically male) approach to seeking answers to life's questions, the number 11 is believed to resonate on a higher spiritual plane. In some quarters 11 is linked with the planet and goddess Venus, whereas the number 7 is linked to the planet and god Mars. The master number 22 is considered to expand consciousness, having the characteristics of intuition, illumination, and enlightenment. Hence, eleven-circuit labyrinths, such as the one in Chartres Cathedral, as well as the larger stone labyrinths found across Finland and Sweden, would naturally hold such appeal within cultures in which the magic of numbers was an accepted part of life.

Church designers were very adept at integrating the labyrinth symbol, irrespective of how little space they had to work with. It is believed that the smallest church labyrinth appears on a wall at Lucca Cathedral in Italy, being only 19½ inches in diameter. The original design incorporated a representation of Theseus and the Minotaur (as did the original Chartres design) but the friction caused by many thousands of tracing fingers has erased this.

Excellent variations of the medieval Christian labyrinth cannot only be found at Chartres (on the rare occasions when the church authorities move the chairs that frequently cover it) but also at Amiens and Bayeux cathedrals. Unfortunately, many splendid examples have been destroyed in the intervening years, including the labyrinth at Rheims Cathedral, which was laid down in blue marble in 1240 but was deliberately destroyed over 500 years later by a certain Canon Jacquemart who disliked having to compete with the noise made by children and others who walked the labyrinth during services.

The eleven-circuit labyrinth at Chartres Cathedral.

The smallest church labyrinth appears at Lucca Cathedral, Italy. It originally contained an image of Theseus and the Minotaur but this has worn away over the years.

This octagonal labyrinth is to be found in Amiens Cathedral.

The tree-like labyrinth design at Poitiers Cathedral was destroyed many years ago.

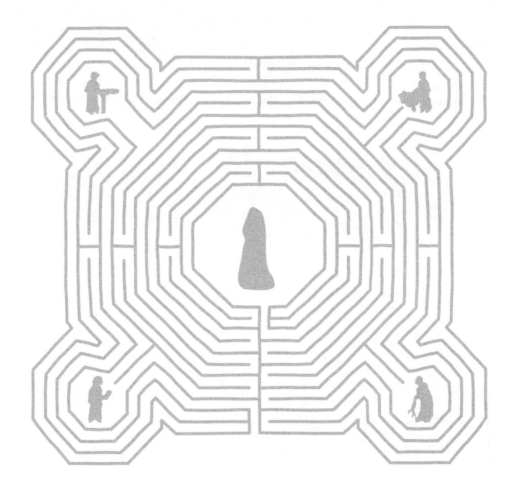

The Rheims Cathedral labyrinth with its distinctive four "bastions" was laid down in blue marble in 1240. It was destroyed in the eighteenth century.

Like the Rheims Cathedral labyrinth, the turf labyrinth at Saffron Walden in Britain has four "bastions," although in this case they are rounded.

Labyrinths in Sens and Auxerre Cathedrals, among others, were similarly demolished, including the intriguing example at Poitiers Cathedral which was tree-like in its design. A particular favorite of mine is the turf labyrinth on the common at Saffron Walden in Britain which is reminiscent of the Rheims design in that – although round instead of diamond-shaped – it also has four "bastions."

One of the ways in which the Chartres labyrinth is unique is that the "turns" directed towards the north, east and west of the pattern look like hour glasses. In an eleven-circuit labyrinth, there are ten of these markings, known as "labrys."

Labrys

The labrys is the double-headed axe symbol that was found in abundance – as engravings, bronze models, and set into pedestals – during the excavation of the palace at Knossos in Crete by Sir Arthur Evans (1851–1941).

The double-headed axe symbol known as the "labrys."

The palace of King Minos was probably built between 2000 and 1500 B.C., although the Minoan civilization was flourishing on Crete over 500 years earlier. This 35,000ft square building was a maze of interlinking passages and is the setting for the mythical story of Theseus and the Minotaur (*see* page 66). One room – a hall some 80ft by 26ft – is known as "the Hall of the Double Axes" because of the large number of labrys symbols appearing there.

Why, if the labyrinth derives both from this word and hence the shape of the Cretan double-headed axe, is there no indication of this symbol in the Classical seven-circuit labyrinth? So far the labrys shape has only been discerned within the design of the much later Chartres labyrinth. This is one of those occasions where several concepts have become – erroneously – intertwined. There is no historical basis for linking the labrys with the labyrinth, except that it was a neat way of explaining the supposed derivation of a word and a symbol. It is probable that the Chartres pattern incorporated turns to divide the circle into quadrants in order to relate to the seasons or the church calendar, and it was some time later that someone noticed that the shapes that had been produced by this resembled the Cretan double-headed axe.

Indeed, on the Lucca inscription (*see* page 5) the word we spell "labyrinth" was spelled "laberinth" by the Romans. Even later, the seventeenth-century Yorkshire diarist Abraham de la Pryme refers to the Roman games from which labyrinths got their name "Troy Towns" (*see* page 3) as being played in "great labarinths cut upon the ground." It appears that the tendency to spell this word with a "y" was a much later custom. Also, the word labrys is spelled with the "y" coming after the "r," whereas with the word labyrinth they are the other way around. So, it is doubtful whether a link between the labyrinth and the labrys symbols is anything other than wishful thinking. The labrys symbol, considerably older than Minoan, is linked with the mythical race of female warriors, the Amazons, reputed to have come from north-eastern Turkey. Suggestive of the inner vaginal lips of labia minora, the double-headed axe is said to have been carried by women as a scepter and a weapon.

Some reports suggest that the double axe was used over 8,000 years ago as an agricultural tool – a scythe – at the world's oldest-known settlement, Catal Huyuk, in central Turkey. Certainly, the labrys is associated strongly with goddess worship and the matrifocal tribes that flourished in Caria in Asia Minor and for this reason the symbol was acquired by lesbian communities during the 1970s and has appeared on many of their accoutrements ever since.

Lunations

It is also worth making a brief mention of another unique feature of the Chartres labyrinth – the scallop-like patterns called "lunations." These partial circles are only found on the circumference of this particular design and number 28.5 part-circles known as "foils" and 28 points or "cusps," for each of the four quadrants – 113 foils in total. Some suggest that the Chartres labyrinth doubled as a calendar, denoting the 28-day lunar cycle. As Dr. Lauren Artress of Grace Cathedral points out, this particular design is not complete without the addition of the lunations and no matter how challenging they are to incorporate accurately, she believes they have an important part to play in the overall energetic quality of the Chartres labyrinth.

Roman Mosaics

A further labyrinth pattern grouping deserves mention – that of the Roman mosaics. Mosaics are pictures and patterns built up by joining together small pieces of glass, marble, or other colored, hard materials. The word "mosaic" is derived from an ancient Greek term relating to the Muses, the nine Greek goddess of inspiration. This art form is believed to have originated in the third century by the Greeks, who used colored pebbles, although it was soon discovered that this was a useful way of using pieces of broken or sub-standard pottery.

In Roman households, these robust floor coverings were the equivalent of our carpets, only they could be personalized to convey a message about the occupation and status of the building's occupants. Roman labyrinth mosaics are invariably square given their practical purpose, with the same pattern repeated in quadrants to cover a floor or piazza. Square labyrinths also featured in other cultures, for example the Hopi symbol for Mother Earth is square – although there is no direct correlation between the two patterns, other than their shape.

The Romans were particularly fond of incorporating scenes of Theseus slaying the Minotaur in the center of their labyrinths (*see* page 66), a device that also featured in many later church pavement labyrinths, including Chartres. A particularly impressive Roman mosaic labyrinth, featuring additional panels describing scenes from that adventure, was discovered in Salzburg, Austria and is now displayed in the Kunsthistorisches Museum in Vienna.

The Changing Shape of Labyrinths

The more one explores the labyrinths of antiquity the more it becomes apparent that this is a dynamic pattern – ever-changing and evolving, only bounded by the limits of humankind's creativity. Some labyrinths, like the Hopi symbol for Mother Earth, are square. At Amiens Cathedral, the labyrinth is octagonal. A 20ft-square version near the west door of Ely Cathedral, laid down in 1870, is diamond shaped with four additional sections protruding from each of the four sides. Labyrinths have been created to look like a winding snake – a sort of extension on the snakes and ladder's children's game (without the ladders!). Other, contemporary examples, have been laid out to look like a goddess (the center being the head) with her flowing hair and outstretched arms becoming the pathways.

And the creativity continues. US labyrinth designer, Dr. Alex Champion produces earthworks reminiscent of the Serpent Mound in Ohio – the 1,250ft-long Native American prehistoric monument constructed by tribes living in the Mississippi Valley. Each year he comes up with more meander designs, not necessarily unicursal, but offering many different routes through which to move from the entrance to the center – just no dead ends. What makes Alex Champion's earthworks so intriguing is that the pathways are trenches with the earth mounded up, frequently knee high.

On his property in Mendocino County, California, Alex Champion has produced five interpretations of the labyrinth, each one with pathways barely one-person wide that require you to

One of Alex Champion's modern labyrinth earthwork designs.

become more deliberate in your steps. Some of the patterns incorporate interesting little details, such as mosaic inlays and rocks embedded in the mounds.

Most recently, Lea Goode-Harris, a fifth-generation Californian with a connection to the earth through her family's roots in grape growing and winemaking, created a new labyrinth design named after her hometown of Santa Rosa. While researching ancient labyrinths, Lea became inspired to draw a version that is quite unlike any other. The Santa Rosa labyrinth differs from the Chartres design in that it comprises seven rather than eleven circuits, the entrance pathway is directly in line with the exit, and there is a neat little altar or "heart" space, four circuits in. Constructed single-handedly in a corner of her garden, Lea's labyrinth comprises the turf walk-ways, each divided by a single row of embedded bricks. The perimeter is circumscribed by red bricks and Lea has placed a silver orb balanced on a stone pedestal in the center of the labyrinth and this catches the sun and moonlight in interesting ways.

Lea Goode-Harris' latest project is an artistic creation that will connect people to nature at the new Charles M. Schultz Museum in Santa Rosa. Jean F. Schultz, the wife of the late creator of the Peanuts comic strip, had heard Lea talk about labyrinths and contacted her to ask if she might be able to create a labyrinth in the shape of Snoopy's head. In Lea's words, "To the music of the Peanuts gang and a little Snoopy image before me, the meandering paths of the contemporary Snoopy Labyrinth emerged from my creative imagination."

Lea Goode-Harris' seven-circuit Santa Rosa design.

THE GEOMETRY OF LIFE

What is it about the circle that is so universally compelling? This ancient symbol continues to resonate in the minds, hearts and spirits of humanity and if you were to ask a group of people to make spontaneous doodles, the majority of these – the sun, concentric circles, spirals, smiley faces, serpents biting their own tails – would in some way relate to a circular theme.

Circles are found among the very earliest human expressions of art and communication. In the High Neolithic period of the Near East (4500–3500B.C.), a variety of geometric shapes appeared on pottery and other artifacts – symbols such as the swastika, the Maltese cross and the double-headed axe (the "labrys," from which the labyrinth is reputed to get its name) – all contained in circular borders. The entrance to the 5,500 year-old megalithic tomb at Newgrange in Ireland features a huge stone into which concentric circles were chipped with flint tools.

Spirals and circles carved into the entrance of the 5,500 year-old megalithic tomb of Newgrange, Ireland.

The wheel-like sun cross — a circle divided into four equal wedges by the insertion of a cross — appears on Bronze Age rock carvings from China to pre-Columbian America and the Middle East. This symbol is said to represent the highest power and complete control. When Wiccans "cast the circle," they are creating a sacred space inside which their ritual work can be conducted with the greatest energy and power. And the Medicine Wheel of Native Americans and the Plains Indians of Alberta, Canada, is not just of astrological significance, but a psycho-spiritual tool whereby the four directions represent the lifelong quest to incorporating the realms of the physical, mental, spiritual, and psychological. If you compare the classical Cretan-style labyrinths with the medieval Christian design you will see that the latter, through its quadrants, highlights the cruciform pattern associated with the Christian faith.

One particularly impressive example of a medicine wheel can be found close to the summit of the Big Horn Mountains in Wyoming, after which it is named. The Big Horn medicine wheel is thought to have been built by one of the tribes that hunted nearby — possibly the Crow, Cheyenne or Arapaho. It is a 100-foot-wide wheel made of boulders and it closely resembles the design of the sun-dance lodges constructed by the Cheyenne during their sacred sun rituals. Like the standing stone circles or "henges" of Britain — such as Stonehenge, the Rollrights, and the Callanish on the Isle of Lewis in Scotland — all the circular prehistoric monuments have relationships with the phases of the sun or moon and hence, probably, the tides.

One contemporary Native American group, the Sun Bear Tribe Medicine Society, has blended the spiritual wisdom symbolized by the "Great Wheels" with that of non-native Oriental motifs such

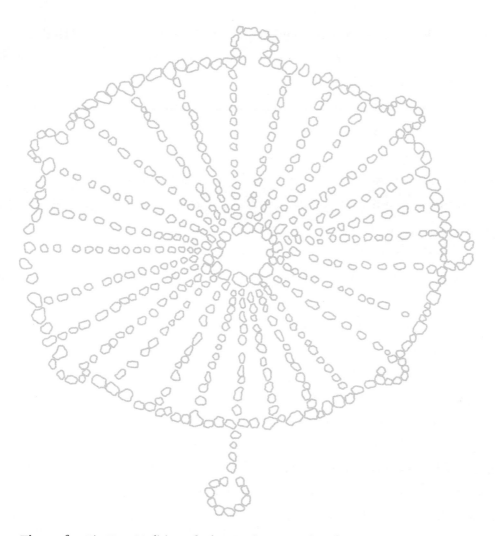

The 100-foot Big Horn Medicine Wheel, Wyoming. It may have been used in sacred sun rituals.

as the mandala. The word "mandala" means "circle" or "wheel" in Sanskrit. Mandalas are used by Buddhists and many New Age followers as an aid to meditation. Sand mandalas, created to demonstrate the cosmos, and the impermanence of everything that exists within it, are made by Navajo Indians as well as Tibetan monks. These intricate spiritual art forms are produced from crushed, colored crystals and semi-precious stones and, because of the intricacy of their construction, they can take many days to complete. They are then swept away as part of a special ritual or ceremony. Because of the Navajo superstition that bad luck would befall anyone who did not ceremoniously destroy these sand paintings, it was not until the 1930s that they began to be woven into textiles.

The Wheel of Life, the Tibetan representation of the cyclical process of life and the different realms of existence, frequently appears on similarly detailed Tibetan and Nepalese art or *thankas*. Because of the time and attention that goes into producing these carefully painted pictures, each takes one or two years to complete. The *thankas* invariably incorporate other geometric shapes within their overall design, but are always framed by an outer circle. As with the labyrinth, the yin–yang symbol and the patterns found in nature that can be used to invoke a meditative state, mandalas and medicine wheels are basically circular with a clearly denoted center.

The concept of the circle covers a wide range of meanings – containment, completeness, unity, infinity, the Sun and the Moon, cyclic motion, potentiality, resurrection, the Wheel of Life – life without end. The circle represents both something and nothing – pure potential within a fixed boundary. This is an intriguing metaphor for the apparent paradox of free will and destiny. Within the circle of life we have complete freedom to select whatever pathways compel us most (or choose to have that selection dictated to us by others) while being bounded by a specific sphere of influence and activity in the form of gender, race, socio-economic status or family background.

The circle is a frequent pattern in nature – both sub-atomically and visibly. Photographed in a bubble chamber, the tracks of subatomic particles are shown to be distinctively spiral. And the sound waves produced by chanting the sacred word "Om" have been found to produce circular patterns when passed through sand. A pebble, thrown into water, causes the water to flow in concentric circles and phenomena such as whirlpools and tornadoes take on the form of a vortex.

There are many other examples of circular or labyrinthine forms within the human body itself. Crooke's *Body of Man* refers to "the labyrinthine mazes and web of the small arteries." The intestines are a mass of labyrinthine tubes and the birth canal might be thought of as akin to a unicursal maze – albeit "one way." The innermost part of the ear, resembling a snail's shell, is known as the labyrinth, and certain variations of the labyrinth design, such as the Santa Rosa pattern (*see* page 49), are reminiscent of a cross section of the human brain. Externally, the whorls on fingerprints are also similar to labyrinth circuits.

Sacred Geometry

The nautilus shell is a wonderful example of the mathematical symmetry found in the natural world – as the spiral grows along equally spaced axes, its proportions are structured according to certain arithmetical sequences. "Transcendal" patterns like these are part of the discipline of sacred geometry, which examines and demonstrates the link between the human spirit and its physical environment. The application of sacred geometry is like tuning a musical instrument so that it resonates at the right frequency to produce the required harmonious note. In the case of a labyrinth designed according to sacred geometry, that frequency is healing energy that acts at the metaphysical level.

Sacred geometry is not the easiest concept to explain in words, being much easier to illustrate as a sensation or experience. It can also seem somewhat cumbersome and complex to those of us who found ourselves befuddled by mathematics at school. Our ancestors not only ascribed mystical

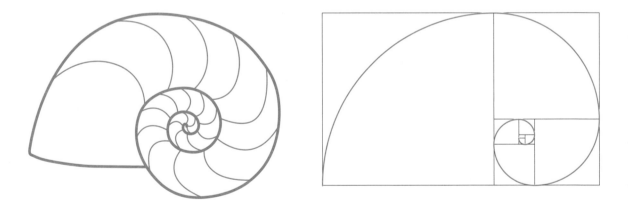

Many shapes in nature follow arithmetic sequences. Here we see how the shape of a Nautilus shell follows the Fibonacci sequence, the geometric ratio of which grows ever closer to the Golden Mean (1.6180).

and healing properties to certain geometric forms – especially the circle – they also recognized that nature's shapes followed certain arithmetical ratios. One of the best known is the Fibonacci series, named after the Italian mathematician Leonardo Fibonacci (1170–1250A.D.). He discovered a strong tendency for natural occurrences to follow a particular numerical sequence, whether it concerns the breeding patterns of rabbits or the family trees of honeybees. Each number in the sequence is the sum of the previous two – 1, 1, 2, 3, 5, 8, 13, 21, 34 … As this sequence continues beyond 8 and 13, the pairings are in a ratio closer and closer to a special number known as the Golden Mean (1.6180). The Golden Mean is a ratio that is found in the growth patterns of many plants. For example, if you take a bird's-eye view of the way that leaves are arranged around a stem you will notice that the pattern ensures that there is some distance between any leaf that lies directly above a lower one. This ensures that the sun and rain are not prevented from reaching the lower leaves. The number of leaves in a rotation before this happens is invariably a Fibonacci number.

The Golden Mean has long been considered a "transcendental number", a word that speaks strongly to our sense of spiritual well-being – even enlightenment. Long before the ancient Greeks calculated special ratios such as this, or Fibonacci gave his name to the sequence, our ancestors seemed to have understood that there is a symmetry in nature that produces a certain state of consciousness. The ancient Greeks and Egyptians followed this natural law of geometry and applied the Golden Ratio in the designs of their most important buildings, monuments, and temples. Numerology, including the numbers 7 and 11, together with sacred geometry, helped them construct buildings that reflected the natural laws governing patterns in nature. Ancient monuments such as the pyramids of Egypt or the Parthenon, or later constructions such as the Taj

Mahal or an Armenian church, have a harmonious feel about them that is ineffable, but peaceful and uplifting. They are both easy on the eye and on the soul. That is the power of nature's numbers.

Today, mathematicians are turning their attention to "fractals," the more complicated geometric shapes found in nature. The shape of ferns, landscapes, clouds, and coastlines are said to be fractal because of the infinite amount of detail involved in them. For example, when you approach a coastline by sea it looks like a straight line from a distance. However, it soon becomes apparent that this supposed line has a multitude of indentations. And as you get closer and closer – until you are standing on the beach with a microscope, discerning each grain of sand – you discover more and more indentations and extrusions, curvatures that were previously unimagined.

THE SITING OF LABYRINTHS

Earth Energies

Feng Shui is founded on the importance of living in harmony with both visible and invisible earth energies. In order to live a happy, healthy, fortuitous life – according to Feng Shui principles – you need to locate your home and undertake your activities close to an auspicious balance of natural forces. Natural features such as hills and mountains were considered beneficial in ancient China, from where Feng Shui has its roots, blocking the straight lines along which evil spirits or the negative energy (*sha*) were supposed to travel. Beijing, for example, was built on plains surrounded on three sides by mountains, thereby protecting it from danger. An artificial stream was constructed in the southern part in order to balance opposing forces representing fire and water. Ancient Chinese geomancers would look carefully at the shape and alignments of hills, valleys and plains in order to ascertain whether there was an implied shape of an animal or bird – clues as to the type of invisible energy operating there.

The ancient Hindus had an equivalent "dwelling science" known as Vastu Vidya which offers practical ways in which to design or re-arrange a home or workplace. Again, the goal is to balance the *gunas* (forces of energy) that pervade all things, animate or inanimate, in order that the greatest fortune and well-being could be assured.

Hence, thousands of years before the splitting of the atom, geomancers, shamans, and pagan societies understood that everything we perceive as "solid" is really energy vibrating at different rates. Indeed, in "energy medicine," an umbrella term which includes therapies such as homeopathy and Bach flower remedies, Reiki, crystal healing, shiatsu and acupuncture, healing and disease are said to occur at the sub-biochemical, energetic level.

Many of us have experienced an uplifting, almost transcendental feeling when we have visited certain "special" spots – whether areas of natural beauty or buildings constructed according to ancient geomancy principles, as were the Parthenon and the ancient theatre of Dionysus, in Athens. If you have ever felt a strange fluttering in your abdomen or heart as you approach an ancient monument, or gasped in awe as you gazed over a particularly beautiful landscape, then you will have some appreciation of the way in which natural laws governing pattern and form enhance the art of harmonious living by stirring the spirit.

Dowsing

Clearly, the choice of location for a labyrinth should not be an arbitrary decision. Many labyrinth creators or community project leaders ensure they place their labyrinth in the most beneficial place possible by calling on the services of a professional dowser to check – among other things – the compatibility of the space they have selected with the positioning and design of the labyrinth they have chosen. Dowsing attracts mixed reviews and it is for you to decide whether this is something you wish to explore further before siting your own labyrinth.

Dowsing is an ancient intuitive art, the most well known branch of which is known as rhabdomancy or water divining, but its use extends much further than this. Dowsers use sticks (often willow or hazel), swinging rods (which can be made easily from coat-hanger wire and the casings of ballpoint pens) or some kind of pendulum to detect energy signals. The essence of the practice is that you program the rod or pendulum to move in a particular direction in the presence of whatever it is you are dowsing for. As in crystal healing, the "battery power" is provided by thought, energy or intention.

For example, in the case of deciding where to situate a labyrinth for optimum healing energy you would begin by relaxing into a meditative state. Your attention then becomes divided between the external environment and your internal sensitivity. It is in this state that you would focus on your ultimate intention for building a labyrinth – this is really all about directing healing energy, both for the environment on which it is built, and for those who walk it.

Dowsers suggest that the first question you ask at the site of your proposed labyrinth is "May we site a labyrinth here?," asking permission of the earth spirits and tapping into their wisdom as to whether a labyrinth would benefit that place. If the answer is "no," then it is not worth wasting your time as the energy would not be right. If the answer is "yes," you would then formulate a series of closed questions which simply require a yes/no response from the dowsing instrument you are using. Such a question might be: "Should the entrance to this labyrinth face east?" in which case you would walk slowly in that general direction, over the area where the proposed labyrinth entrance would be situated – and observe the instrument's response.

Questions to ask

Bearing in mind the importance of siting a labyrinth in accordance with the energies of a particular place, here is a checklist of questions to ask yourself before you begin. Should you choose not to dowse the area before laying out your labyrinth, I strongly advise that you meditate beforehand – perhaps using a finger labyrinth as a meditative tool (*see* Resources page 174). (If you are dowsing, change the wording of these questions so they can be answered by yes/no responses.) Focus on each of the following questions in turn, and trust your intuition. You will know whether any decision feels right or not.

- *How appropriate is it for you to locate your labyrinth in this particular spot? Does the energy of this place feel conducive to positioning this spiritual tool here?*
- *What design and materials are you most attracted to and are these in keeping with your chosen environment?*
- *Is there an existing feature that you wish to incorporate into the center of your labyrinth and how will this tree, bush, flowerbed, or rock contribute to the energies of this space?*
- *What is the maximum diameter that your space can accommodate for the labyrinth, given that walkers will need freedom to walk around the perimeter before and after their meditation?*
- *Towards which direction should the entrance to your labyrinth face, bearing in mind things such as light (day and night), the surrounding landscaping and its view, and other natural features?*
- *Do you wish your labyrinth to be positioned in accordance with the equinoxes or solstices and how will this affect its position?*
- *Are there water pipes or large water features nearby that might affect or be affected by the energy of the labyrinth? (See page 141 for a relevant story.)*

A lot of ground has been covered in this chapter, particularly around how the patterns of labyrinths and the patterns in nature can produce a transcendental experience because of the special qualities ascribed to numbers, ratio, and form. When planning and making a labyrinth, nowhere does it say that your labyrinth has to be big or lavishly decorated.

What is most important is that you get a sense of the best site for your labyrinth – you create one that fits easily into your lifestyle and its design speaks to you. For example, if you are a city dweller, you could make or buy a wooden or plastic finger labyrinth and trace it every morning as a precursor to your daily life and before you go to sleep at night. Alternatively, you could reproduce a miniature Cretan labyrinth in a window box, using pebbles or shells that remind you of a special holiday, or large, brightly colored beads. Even a small garden can have a labyrinth — remember that it can have just three pathways rather than seven. Later in the book we will look at ways other people have incorporated labyrinths into their lives and how you can use similar ideas, scaled down, according to the space, money, and time you have available.

For now, we are going to explore the psychological benefits of walking, tracing or meditating on the labyrinth symbol and how this will free you from the constraints of the "maze mind."

chapter 3

EMERGING FROM THE MAZE MIND

Like hoodwinked fools, perplex'd we grope our way,
And during life's short course we blindly stray, Puzzled
in mazes and perplex'd with fears.

"REFLECTIONS ON WALKING IN THE MAZE AT HAMPTON COURT" — ANON, 1747

The labyrinth motif has been found as rock carvings, on coins, and pre-Christian and medieval artwork as well as pavement and finger meditation tools within Gothic churches. Today, all manner of labyrinthine designs are springing up around the world, with all kinds of applications. All these have one thing in common: regardless of the intricacy of the design, from the simple Classical seven-circuit labyrinth, to the more formal, Roman mosaic patterns and the highly ornate, medieval Christian examples seen at Chartres and Amiens cathedrals, labyrinths have a single, inevitable route to the center.

MAZES AND LABYRINTHS

However, the most well-known of labyrinth stories, Theseus and the Minotaur, features a multi-cursal structure which today we would term a maze – one in which a monster has been contained within its diabolical design. This presents our hero with similar challenges faced by each of us at some time in our lives – psychologically if not physically. Firstly, there is the acceptance or refusal of one of life's challenges that, in the case of Theseus, was freely sought and undertaken. Secondly, having found the courage with which to journey into the darkness one must confront the Shadow archetype – typically symbolized as a monstrous beast like the Minotaur – and face metaphorical, if not literal, death. And thirdly, having faced those fears with heroic determination and ingenuity, the hero emerges resurrected and forever changed by the experience. As you will discover, the labyrinth symbol can provide a psychological tool with which to navigate life's journey more successfully and joyfully.

Ancient Greek mythology is richly painted with universal patterns or "archetypes" that remain true for us today. The inner focus that shaped the lives and adventures of deities such as Zeus, Athena, and Demeter are symbolically illustrative of the collective human experience – embracing, among others, emotions such as anger and avarice, courage and compassion, generosity and grief. These stories have remained alive because they relate to attitudes, behaviors, and emotions that transcend the barriers of time and space. What these ancient Greek storytellers were so adept at doing was identifying unconscious patterns in the way human beings act out their lives.

The Theseus story illustrates the distinction between what constitutes a maze and a labyrinth. A maze is a puzzle with dead ends, false turns, and "red herrings." It has been likened to a game of chess in which the designer plays all his moves in advance and whose purpose it is to challenge the participants to win the game by reaching the center. Supposedly, the more diabolical the puzzle, the more fun is the game.

A labyrinth, on the other hand, offers a direct route to the center and simply requires you to retrace your steps to get back out. Thus, the challenge is an illusion when looked at it from the outside, because all that is required is to keep putting one foot in front of the other and to have faith that the goal will eventually be reached. However, this was not the challenge confronting Theseus.

Theseus and the Minotaur

Theseus, a mortal, was the son of Aegeus, king of Athens. He was brought up by his mother, Aethra, in a town called Troizen (another possible reason for the naming of labyrinths as "Troy Towns," *see* page 4). Demonstrating some similarity to the story of young Arthur, king of the Britons, Aegeus had left his sword under a huge boulder with the instructions that when the boy was strong enough to remove it, he should join his father in Athens which, in the roundabout way of mythology, he eventually did.

Across the waters in Crete, King Minos had problems of his own. Following a disagreement between Minos and the Sea God, Poseidon, the king's wife, Pasiphae, had become pregnant by a

Theseus and the Minotaur depicted in the labyrinth at Knossos.

magnificent white bull. Thus she gave birth to the Minotaur, half man, half bull, a creature so terrifying and unmanageable that Minos commissioned a Greek architect named Daedalus to design a maze cunning enough that the monster should never be able to escape from it – nor anyone else .

Now, King Minos held a grudge against the people of Athens, where his son, Androgeus, had been gored to death by a bull. His revenge was to order King Aegeus to send him seven young men and seven young women every nine years so that they could be sacrificed to the terrible Minotaur. Theseus persuaded his father, the King, to make him one of the seven males, promising to kill the monster and put an end to this ghastly tribute. The king reluctantly agreed, stipulating that if Theseus was successful he should return to Athens showing a white sail on his boat, rather than the customary black sail. Theseus agreed, and set sail for Knossos with his thirteen hapless companions.

To complicate matters for Minos, the King's daughter – Ariadne – fell madly in love with Theseus, upon arrival. This is where the story gets a little hazy as to whether the victims were to enter the maze alone or as a group. But in any event, Ariadne was determined to save her heart's desire from a terrible fate and forced Daedalus, the designer of the maze, to tell her how Theseus might escape after killing the Minotaur.

The answer lay in a simple ball of yarn that Theseus was told to unravel as he entered and passed through the puzzling passages. In true hero style, he found the foul creature and killed it. By following the yarn back through the maze, Theseus easily reached the exit and escaped, with Ariadne and the other Athenians – destination Athens.

The Crane Dance

According to legend, Theseus and his party stopped off at the island of Delos, a sacred sanctuary being known as the birthplace of the god Apollo and his twin sister, Artemis. There the group performed the first Geranos *or "Crane Dance." This involved making crane-like movements as if one was stepping through a labyrinth, and the dance thereafter become a custom engaged in by the inhabitants of that Mediterranean island. There are three parts to the Delian festival Crane Dance, each highly suggestive of the labyrinth design. The* strophe *movements go from right to left, while the* antistrophe *movements go from left to right. The final part, reminiscent of the period of calm in the center of the labyrinth, is called the* stationary, *when slower movements were conducted before the altar.*

The crane was the sacred bird of Mercury/Hermes, the messenger of the Gods and rock carvings found at Val Camonica in northern Italy, estimated to have been made around 1800–1300B.C., depict a crane standing close by a classical Cretan-style labyrinth. Demonstrating yet another link with the area where shamanism originated (see page 12), an eighteenth-century traveler to Russia discovered that the Ostiaks of western Siberia would dress themselves up in the skins of cranes for their own elaborate Crane Dance. The reason that cranes dance in the wild may be significant to the altered state of consciousness attributed to walking the labyrinth — these birds only do it when they are happy. There is no element of aggression in these flapping and leaping movements as with many other birds; indeed, ornithologists point out that the dancing of cranes indicates that they are comfortable in their surroundings and that they have a strong relationship with other, nearby cranes. While crane dancing in nature occurs as a sign of exuberance, it is particularly common in the spring, as the birds engage in their mating rituals.

Crane dances are common across many cultures to which this water bird is a native. In Korea, the Dongnae Crane Dance is carried out at festivals whereby the dancers imitate the acrobatic motions of joyful cranes. This type of abandoned dance has been a feature of Aboriginal folklore for thousands of years. Plus, on the other side of the world, members of the Sauk and Mesquakie tribes of Mississippi engaged in a two- or three-day Crane Dance during which young braves would make entreaties to the women they wished to marry.

In these carvings from Val Camonica, northern Italy, a crane, the sacred bird of Mercury/ Hermes, is seen standing by a Cretan-style labyrinth.

Unfortunately, the conclusion to the pairing of Theseus and Ariadne is not so joyful and the destinies of other characters in this story are short-lived. Our fickle hero abandoned the loyal Ariadne *en route* to Athens and she later married the god Dionysus, and through that association became connected with the Corona Borealis or Northern Crown, a pattern of stars that resembles the front legs of a spider.

Ariadne's story is a telling example of young lust or obsession with an unsuitable partner. The princess' destiny was far greater than to be with a mere mortal – she was to be the consort of a god. So while she and Theseus were destined to meet so that she could save him, this was to be the extent of their relationship. The gods had another, much grander purpose for her than to be left alone while our hero went off on more adventures – as Theseus did, after reaching home and becoming King of Athens. And she was probably too good for him, not just because he abandoned her when she was no longer of any use to him, but he thoughtlessly forgot to change the color of his sail when his boat returned to Athens. Upon seeing a black sail, his father thought his son had died, and Aegeus then threw himself into the sea and drowned. The Aegean is named after the old king.

Daedalus also suffered. He was imprisoned with his son Icarus for his role in Theseus' escape. The Greek designer cleverly constructed a set of wings held together by wax for himself and Icarus so they could fly to safety. But the impetuous boy – typical teenager – did not listen to his father, flew too near to the sun and his wings fell apart. Icarus plunged to his death, although Daedalus escaped.

On one level, the Theseus myth may be interpreted as indicating that before receiving divine guidance (and, remember, Ariadne was a deity on her mother's side) life seems like a never-ending puzzle, full of promising avenues that result in frequent disappointment when they turn out to be dead ends.

On another level, the story suggests that a wholly logical approach is inappropriate for a spiritual quest. The key to unlocking the secrets of the Knossos labyrinth may have been devised by a man (Daedalus, the architect) but was delivered by a woman (Ariadne), representing intuition. This means learning to trust our inner knowledge and letting go of the apparent safety of a rational approach. This story is also illustrative of the successful outcome achieved when male and female energy – the yin and yang of ancient Chinese symbolism – combine.

The Helping Goddess

Mythological heroes are frequently assisted by goddesses, rather than by their male coun-
terparts. Athena was the mentor and supporter of Achilles and Ulysses. The Egyptian god-
desses Isis and Nephthys rescued King Osiris who then became Lord of the Underworld. In
Celtic mythology, the triple goddesses known as the Morrigan, were invoked by warriors
before they went into battle. And gentler heroes call upon the Muses, originally nine pre-
Greek wilderness goddesses, who bestow inspiration upon writers, poets, and artists of all
kind. The concept of one or more powerful female figures is found in all cultures, although
the means by which the goddess wields that power differs. For example, the Hindu goddess
Kali Ma – another example of virgin birth (see page 24) is a ferocious creature whose role
is to rid the world of evil demons that try to capture humanity. She is known variously as
the Dark Mother and the Destroyer and is frequently pictured standing over the body of her
consort, Shiva, with his blood and entrails dripping from her gaping mouth.

In contrast, the Chinese goddess Kuan Yin or "Great Mother of China" is worshipped as a
serene and peace-loving deity. According to legend, she defied her father and, refusing to
marry, chose to die rather than give up her childhood desire to be a nun. In the course of her
execution, she heard a human soul cry out and committed herself to stay in this world in
order to relieve all suffering, rather than move up to Heaven. Statues of Kuan Yin are
often found in Chinese homes and she is believed to have the power to heal the sick and rid
people of life's difficulties.

Not surprisingly, the concept of the goddess continues to be worshipped to this day in deference to the fact that she wielded ultimate power over the forces of nature and, in particular, the power of intuition.

The Chinese Goddess Kuan Yin — "She Who Hears the Cries of the World."

THE JOURNEY THROUGH THE LABYRINTH

The labyrinthine journey represents an elegant, satisfying, and insightful approach to life – a single pathway leading to the goal of illumination, wisdom, or enlightenment. Nevertheless, it requires us to demonstrate and benefit from the qualities of courage, endurance, and faith that we learned from our earlier time in the maze. Our earliest ancestors may have related to the unicursal labyrinth with its linear path because they experienced life in a very different way to contemporary existence. Their lives were in harmony with nature; they respected the environment and its delicate balance and were open to its beneficial earth energies. It is no coincidence that the labyrinth motif is analogous to the concept of Kundalini energy. According to ancient Hindu tradition, Kundalini (*see* page 16) remains coiled like a serpent at the base of the spine until the time when it is awakened and rises through the metaphysical body, piercing each energy center or chakra in turn. Upon reaching the crown the subject is said to have reached enlightenment. Similarly, the journey through the labyrinth leads to that inevitable place where, furthest away from the external domain of the ego, one finds true meaning, self-acceptance, and peace.

The trick, then, is to transform the life you lead from a multicursal maze into the equivalent of a unicursal labyrinth in order for it to take on a whole new, more fulfilling perspective. In myth and literature, the key to achieving this is simplicity itself: the acceptance of a piece of advice, a talisman or token, as with Theseus' creative use of a ball of string. But, before you can do this, you must be willing to take the first step and journey with the Self into the unknown.

Labyrinths have been symbolically linked with dark, cavernous, mysterious places and are a metaphor for our internal world, the unconscious. The fourteen hapless Athenians who were sent to die in the Minotaur's lair represent the terror each of us faces at the prospect of confronting a Shadow Self that has been imprisoned deep without our psyche but which must be reintegrated with our Conscious Self. Only then can we become balanced and complete in the way we were originally created to be. Again, this ancient Greek myth illustrates a universal life lesson – that destiny will not be thwarted. As a rite of passage, you either enter the labyrinth of your own free will with courage and faith – as did our hero Theseus – or are forced to do so by life circumstances.

But how does such a voyage – the hero's journey – manifest itself in our lives today and why might it be relevant? To answer that, we will look at one way that storytellers from Homer to Hollywood have used archetypes to craft stories. Alongside, I will relate a contemporary, real-life story.

The Call to Change

The hero's journey has been interpreted in countless ways. We discover it in fairy stories and myths where a change to the status quo, to the hero's everyday life, occurs. Most of us are familiar with the story of Beauty and the Beast. This is a common folktale and it appears in many different forms and adaptations. Practically the same story is known as Grimm's *The Summer and Winter Garden*, and as *The Bear Prince* in Switzerland, *Zelinda and the Monster* in Italy and *The Enchanted Frog* in Germany. The tale goes something like this:

A merchant goes on a journey and promises to bring back each of his three daughters a present. All ask for jewels and finery except his youngest daughter, Beauty, who knows that her father will scarcely be able to afford to meet the wishes of her greedy sisters. She asks for the simplest thing she can think of – a rose. At the end of the merchant's travels, he remembers his favorite daughter's desire and thoughtlessly picks a rose from a castle garden. Immediately he is faced with the garden's owner, the monstrous "Beast," who is incensed by this action and demands that one of the man's daughters comes willingly to the castle to live with him or he will kill the merchant. Not surprisingly, Beauty's sisters turn on her when their father returns with his sad story, pointing out that she is responsible for what has happened. Beauty, a gentle, sweet girl, willingly offers herself up as the Beast's companion – even though she thinks the monster's purpose is to kill her. And so the terrified Beauty arrives at the Beast's castle to honor the pledge her father made. Her ordinary world has been intercepted by the Fates and is changed forever.

April's Story

For April, the call to change was similarly unexpected and unwelcome. April was part of a very successful group of training professionals working for a financial services company. However, as is often the case when economic circumstances take a dive, the "soft-skills" departments such as training and human resources were the first to be cut back. April was part of the downsizing and it took place at a particularly unfortunate time for her personally, as well as professionally. Like many of us, she had lived beyond her means and had little or no savings and a large credit card debt. In addition, cutbacks were being made across the country and it was taking many of her friends six months or more to find new positions. Some had not worked in over a year. As with Beauty, when the call for change came April was terrified because of the major change it would mean for her life.

In both cases – for Beauty and April – the call to begin a new life was forced upon them. We are all changing, physiologically, every single day of our lives. It is the mental constraints we apply to ourselves that make change appear to be so unnatural and frightening. Theseus welcomed the challenge and many brave souls have willingly walked into the dark unknown as he did. Irrespective of how or why the call comes, however, there is no doubt that like the heroes of myth, fairy tale, and movie, you cannot disregard this awakening. Like a chain reaction, once the initial change has been put in motion, there is no turning back. Even Theseus did not have this option, given that the tribute to Minos required the sacrifice of fourteen Athenians, and to suddenly say, "Actually, I've changed my mind, I'm not going," would have done Theseus irreparable harm in the eyes of everyone in that State, detrimentally affecting his future role as their king.

The Trial

The next heroic theme is that of the test – the moment that the first threshold has been crossed. For Dorothy in *The Wizard of Oz* it was setting out on the yellow brick road. For Theseus it was stepping into the labyrinth.

Beauty's test is to leave behind her family and face her fears about being eaten by the Beast. For this she needs considerable courage and resolve. On reaching the castle, she admits to the monster that she finds him ugly but, after a while, Beauty realizes she is not dealing with a low, stupid creature whose physical appearance mirrors a menacing and vile character. The Beast is actually a refined and intelligent being. Over the course of time, she is tested to see whether not only can she bring herself to endure his company, but also to love and subsequently marry him.

For April, the test was also emotional. Directly after being laid off, she entered her own psychological labyrinth and fell into a pit of despair. It was hard to watch this normally bubbly, positive woman being so frightened, especially about her financial situation and how long she could maintain her current lifestyle without a job. April's mood would swing between bouts of uncontrollable sobbing and quite dramatic anger when she would rant and rave about why – having given her heart and soul to that company – she had been treated so badly. As with Beauty, with the passage of time, this overpowering negativity slightly lifted. Neither of these heroes could go back and change what had happened. They had to make the best of it. That was April's biggest test – a particularly challenging one given how much of a control freak she had always been. For her own physical and psychological well-being, April had to accept that she had lost her job but not her life. There were other means of making a living; she just needed to apply some creative thinking to deciding what that might be.

Facing up to Doubt

Beauty's continuing challenge was to receive the Beast in her room every evening at nine o'clock. It wasn't that she did not enjoy his company – she did. He was a wonderful, kind, and generous companion. But every evening he would ask her the same question – would she marry him? And every time Beauty told him that she saw him as nothing more than a good friend, therefore the answer had to be no. She also plucked up the courage to tell the Beast that she sorely missed her father – the only man she had ever loved – and asked that she be allowed to go and visit her family. In exchange for this kindness Beauty promised never to leave the Beast entirely.

Now this is where, as is common in archetypal tales, the hero persona transfers from one character to another. The key doubt that has to be faced is now the Beast's, not Beauty's. He has to be brave and trusting enough to let Beauty make that visit to her family, and believe that she will come back to him as promised.

April's doubt, however, was all her own. She doubted herself and her abilities, she doubted that she had the energy and persistence to find a suitable job in challenging circumstances. And she doubted that she could make the lifestyle sacrifices necessary to make the little money she had last as long as possible. April was so racked with doubt that she agreed to do something she had never considered or been drawn to before. She walked a labyrinth in order to use that walking meditation as a means of helping her reflect on her situation and come up with creative solutions.

Towards Rebirth

When we rejoin Beauty she is back in her father's house. And – guess what – she misses the Beast hugely. Then one night she has a dream in which she finds him lying in his garden, dying, reproaching her for her ingratitude to him. This is more than Beauty's compassionate soul can bear and she berates herself for not agreeing to marry him. After all, she reflects, her sisters have married attractive but altogether stupid, vain, dull and idle men who are making them wholly miserable. Could it be any worse to be with someone who only ever wants her to be happy and was actually a huge joy to be around? Was she so superficial as to be put off by him just because of his grotesque appearance? Beauty speeds back to the castle to tell the Beast about her change of heart, only to find him, as in her dream, lying on the grass weak from starvation. He tells her that he thought he had lost her forever and decided that rather than live without her he would prefer to die.

As in all the best stories, Beauty's love for the Beast transforms him into a handsome prince. While Beauty's rebirth was psychological, the Beast's was physical and – now complete – they live happily ever after.

There was a happy ending for April too. She actually found it easier to simplify her life than she had thought. And, years later, she says she is hugely grateful for the financial lessons she learned from that time. She now lives well within her means, has a growing savings fund and enjoys the flexibility and freedom that being her own boss brings. With support and some practical help, April started her own training consultancy three months after being laid off. In fact, her first client was her old company where senior management had realized that, although they had shed a whole department, they still had some pressing training needs. With hindsight, she says, being laid off was the best thing that ever happened to her and it has changed her life – and her attitude to life – profoundly.

ENTERING THE LABYRINTH

There is no simple technique that will immediately transform your life. Fictional heroes only transform their ordinary existences into spiritual successes after a certain amount of time and a lot of courage and determination. Theseus is a wonderful role model for us all. He offered himself up for the challenge and trusted Ariadne's simple suggestion of using a ball of yarn to navigate in and out of the Minotaur's maze. He had a sense of destiny and knew that the gods would come to his aid. That is the whole point of being tested. Hero status is not conferred on just anyone, and it does not comes easily – otherwise there would be no value in it.

You can use the labyrinth symbol as a meditation tool, a problem-solving technique or simply as a way to calm your body and mind. Remember, it is not necessary to have a full-sized labyrinth to walk on. Each one of us has the space for a small box of sand in which we can trace a labyrinth pattern. If you use the Resources section (*see* page 172) to explore the Internet, you will find many tools to help you incorporate the labyrinth symbol into your life. Indeed, there are a number of websites offering full-screen labyrinths for you to trace with your finger.

Sometimes, when you are on what may seem like a lonely journey, it is inspiring to walk a labyrinth in the company of others. Again, the Resources section details people and places where you can enquire if there is a canvas or pavement labyrinth that is open to the public.

Facing Your Fears

There are no magical quick fixes, but there are a number of valuable, self-exploratory methods that you can use to face your fears and challenge them head on. Such tools could include:

- *Debating the issues with a wise and trusted friend;*
- *Looking forward and committing to goals that move you past your doubts;*
- *Prayer;*
- *Keeping a journal;*
- *Using a labyrinth as a meditation or problem-solving device (see page 82).*

Some of these methods may involve seeking out or accepting help from others, in the nature of heroes of old. After all, where would Theseus be if he had not tapped into the female intuition offered him by Ariadne and accepted her help?

Identifying Your Core Beliefs

One valuable way to disarm an attack of distrust – whether that be a lack of trust in your own abilities or of someone else – is to look for evidence that illustrates the contrary; look for evidence that demonstrates you are wrong in these assumptions. Allow your Higher Self to act as your Private Investigator to delve into the deep recesses of your mind to pull out the relevant connections. All you need to uncover is the core belief that is producing this distrustful, fearful, and doubting mood. Such core beliefs might be:

- *I don't have the strength or capability to change my situation.*
- *I've messed up too many times in the past and it won't be any different now.*
- *I can't trust anybody; everybody always lets me down.*
- *I can't do this on my own; I need someone to take care of me.*

Forming an Intention

Try to catch yourself thinking like this before you enter the labyrinth. Then, enriched by having articulated one or more of your beliefs – the ones responsible for your current negative thinking – formulate a single positive intention or question as you walk into the labyrinth. There is no need to try and force examples from memory; they will come, even if the process takes a few days. Your intention or question might be:

- *Where can I find the strength to get myself through this challenging time?*
- *Show me that I am wrong; that there have been many occasions when I have achieved wonderful things for myself, by myself.*
- *Remind me of all the times when other people have helped and supported me.*
- *Help me remember all those times when I have been there for myself. When I was strong, resilient, and resourceful.*

If you do not get an answer straight away, keep asking. Remember, your persistence and resilience is being put to the test here. Consider recording your labyrinth insights in a daily journal. Writing things down is very powerful, not least because it allows you to review your progress and make connections between events that you might otherwise not see. You could use your journal, for example, to jot down all the negative thoughts that you have had during that day and then explore where these beliefs came from, as well as look at alternative ways of viewing the world and your experiences in it. In that way, your pessimistic and illogical self-talk becomes more balanced.

Taking Action

No one should tell you that this stuff is easy. If it were, there would be no sense of accomplishment and self-pride from undertaking the quest in the first place. Later on (*see* page 97) I relate a personal realization that again links the nature of challenges with the labyrinth pathways. You may find that useful to read through to help you see how valuable this tool can be in articulating the pattern of our thoughts. One important thing never to overlook is the importance of action.

Beauty went back to the castle. April sought out professional advice, contacted her old company and put the seeds of growing her own business in motion. All periods of self-reflection need to be followed with action, when you take all the gifts you have accumulated from your journey and apply this wisdom to your life and the service of others.

Retracing Your Steps

All heroes go back to their homelands after an adventure, this being the mythological equivalent of returning from the center of the labyrinth. By now you should know that it is not appropriate just to walk directly out from the center to the perimeter. There is a further part of the process, which entails retracing your steps in order to give yourself time to think about all the ways in which you can weave this self-actualization into your everyday life (*see* Kathy Doore's story, page 158). Then the new, authentic you discovers that life can be much simpler and straightforward (or, to be more accurate, meandering) than you ever dreamed it could be.

The River of Life

Think about that word "meander" for a moment and consider what it is most commonly applied to – a river or stream. Ponder how effortless that energy flows and how appropriately. The same water will sometimes flow gently and at other times will pour dramatically over a ravine. Sometimes it is crystal clear and at other times the water is so turbulent that it churns up the dirt on the riverbed, becoming brown and cloudy. This is a useful image to meditate on further when you next use the labyrinth. Irrespective of the environment in which it finds itself, the river flows and winds about its course in an effortless way. It does not have to "do," it just "is." This is the ultimate lesson that comes from the meandering labyrinth — that if we all learned to stop getting in our own way and relaxed a lot more, we would reach our destinations, our destinies, with joy.

Next time you face an anxious situation, ask yourself: "What if this were all OK?" and then, like the river, intend that you will ride out the current environment looking for the lessons, not the pain. Also, committing to the labyrinth symbol in whatever ways suit you and your lifestyle is a valuable way of ensuring you maintain the equilibrium necessary for your physical and mental well-being. Instead of only using it as an occasional problem solving or stress-relieving tool, learn how to integrate it seamlessly into your life so that the labyrinth's many gifts are made available to you every day.

chapter 4

THE RELEVANCE OF RITUAL

"Try a thing you haven't done three times — once to get over the fear of doing it, twice to learn how to do it and a third time to figure out if you like it or not."

VIRGIL THOMPSON, COMPOSER AND CRITIC, 1896–1989

ACCEPTING THE CHALLENGE OF CHANGE

If there is one certainty in life it is that we constantly face change. And change — by its very nature — involves some kind of loss. When we are born we lose the safety of our mother's womb; when we "come of age" we have the great wide world to conquer and for this we must loosen certain family ties and prise ourselves away from home comforts. Marriage requires getting used to compromise, which means giving up an independent life whereby you could do whatever you wanted. For those of us over 40, we are suddenly faced with the realization that half of our life has gone and the fear that we may never accomplish our youthful dreams. And then retirement … It is not surprising that many men die soon after giving up full-time, paid work. A great many have made the mistake of embedding their whole identity in their work rather than living a balanced life, where outside activities and family play an equal part in achieving a sense of meaning and purpose. For them, these later years can seem particularly challenging. And in the West, where youth and beauty continue to be worshipped, elderly women find themselves losing out on the respect and reverence accorded their Eastern counterparts, just because they have "lost their looks."

With all this focus on loss, change is inevitably a psychologically challenging concept. It is when our minds become more skewed towards what we have had to give up as opposed to what potential gains a new phase in life will bring, that we become prone to depression. And for all our relative material wealth and physical comforts, depression is at epidemic levels in the world today.

THE USE OF RITUAL

Our ancestors also grew up and grew old and change happened to them too, in addition to their daily struggle for survival. How did they cope? One of the most fundamentally important strategies they employed to preserve some semblance of order and stability in their lives — and hence good mental health — was ritual. Rites, ceremonies, customs, habits, services — call them what you will – they were much more a part of life for previous generations than they are for us today.

But it is not so much change in itself that we fear, but having change imposed on us. So many of us are like those people who rush around on Christmas Eve or the day before someone's birthday party, trying to find a suitable present. We know that the event is going to happen – we just never get into the habit of adequately preparing for it. We frequently fail to be proactive about change, thereby suffering a greater sense of loss because we feel we are losing control over our lives. So many of us turn our grief inwards, locked into a negative spiral around the constant changes in our lives – primarily because we fail to appreciate all the opportunities we are being offered. Without an outlet for all this anger and hurt, we can easily become depressed.

Rites of Passage

Although many families in the West no longer share the dinner table together and church attendances have dropped, particularly in urban areas, ritual continues to be embraced during events such as Christmas, New Year, saints' days and even leaving ceremonies at work. As our ancestors understood, symbolic actions or rituals publicly acknowledge the inevitability and value of change alongside continuity. Because many of these rituals involve communal sharing in the event, each participant derives huge comfort from the fact that they will not face a "rite of passage" alone. We have all experienced something similar after we have described a difficult time in our life and another person has responded with: "Yes, I know just what that feels like, I went through exactly the same anxiety." We felt much better knowing that the experience was not unique to us and that all our fears and troubles are known and understood by others.

In addition to preparing youth for adulthood and adults for elderly or wise-person status, ritual is an important tool in understanding and accepting our mortality. In Bali, for example, death is a community event in which everyone in the village has a part to play, whether preparing food for the festivities or decorating the family home or constructing the tower in which the body is transported to the cemetery. One particularly beautiful Balinese ceremony involves each member of the deceased's immediate family symbolically cutting the string that holds their spirit to the Earth. In this way each of the relatives gives their permission for the soul to move on to the next life. Groups sing and chant together in ancient Sanskrit and by the time the body is cremated, the whole family will have had a chance to come to terms with the loss of life by marking the beginning of the soul's new journey.

In Europe, pre-Christian pagans, and those who embrace this old religion today, celebrated eight festivals throughout the year, many of which were incorporated into the Church calendar. This highlighted the concept of the changing seasons that are mirrored in our own lives. Labyrinths and turf mazes were often part of spring festivals, just one example of the way in which country dwellers celebrated the circle of life. For example, in Britain, a "Troy Town" cut into the turf at St. Martha's Hill near Guildford was a meeting point of local youths and maidens on Good Friday who would "indulge in boisterous celebrations." (What these involved and whether any "fertility issues" came from them is not specified.) Christian festivals such as Easter were originally part of the pagan and agricultural calendar. In the universally recognized Wheel of Life of earlier times, Spring was a time of mating, with celebrations that involved men and women acting out the parts of Spring God and Spring Goddess. The May Day celebrations held at the turf maze known as Julian's Bower (*see* page 3) were undoubtedly linked to the pagan festival of Beltane, from which comes the tradition of crowning the May Queen – a symbol of the Maiden Goddess – and dancing around the Maypole.

Also, the June "treading" of the Shepherd's Ring (*see* page 3) would also have had its origins in the important pagan festival of Midsummer when the Solar King was honored. Being so closely in tune with their environment, everyone appreciated and could anticipate that a time of plenty in summer and autumn would give way to death and rebirth experienced in winter and spring. By publicly recognizing the changing seasons and the opportunities for reflection and transformation that always accompany loss, pagan communities were thus able to accept life changes and view them as positive rather than negative experiences.

Introducing Ritual into Your Life

Incorporating ritual into your own life or into that of your community, even in some small way, is a reminder that while many things change, others stay the same. Your external environment may vary and you may choose to modify certain unhelpful behavior traits, but you will carry with you many of the values and beliefs that have guided you throughout your life.

The May Day celebrations at Julian's Bower, Alkborough, North Humberside, were linked to the pagan festival of Beltane.

There are many ways of experiencing the comforts of ritual in your life; all it requires is the discipline to undertake certain meaningful activities at the same time every day, week, or month. This could take the form of reading an inspirational book, writing a journal or diary, or chanting or praying by a personal altar or sacred space. For example, Julia Cameron, author of *The Artist's Way*, advises starting each day by writing "morning pages," thus emptying one's head of anything – major or minor – that needs to be discharged. Many people I know have found this ritual to be a valuable means of dumping their psychological garbage, as well as being an immensely satisfying creative exercise. However, present-day rituals, like their earlier counterparts, should be communal as well as an individual and personal experiences. Joining groups that meet at a regular time and at a regular place is a form of ritual that embraces, variously, the celebration of shared talents – as in a choir, acting ensemble or art class – or an expression of shared values and service to others through community efforts.

The Labyrinth as a Pilgrimage

Walking the labyrinth is a form of ritual. It is a public expression of a private state, that of being on a journey and seeking a more profound understanding of your contribution in the universal tapestry of life. Although the word "pilgrimage" is unfavorably linked with a religious experience, the practice is not tied to any particular creed. People make pilgrimages to different places for all kinds of reasons. Indeed, holidaying in the same beautiful part of France or making an annual visit to Machu Picchu in Peru could be said to be a pilgrimage – somewhere you go to refresh yourself physically, mentally and spiritually.

One possible reason why so many labyrinths were incorporated into Christian churches (and why they were often called "Voyages to Jerusalem") was so that the very young or infirm could undertake a pilgrimage at least once in their life without making a lengthy and exhausting trip abroad. It has even been suggested that it was common practice for medieval pilgrims to crawl around a Chartres labyrinth, and the two hours it might have taken on their knees represents the time it took for Jesus Christ to journey from Pontius Pilate's palace to Calvary. Indeed, when the Venerable Edward Trollope, Archdeacon of Stow produced what is reputed to be the UK's first comprehensive research on the subject of mazes and labyrinths in the UK, published in the *Archaeological Journal* in 1858, he reproduced a drawing of penitents crawling around the labyrinth of St. Anne's Hill in Nottingham. However, as W.H. Matthews pointed out, both the sketch and the conclusion about it that Dr. Trollope made were based on conjecture and no direct evidence of this practice exists.

Pilgrimage – the opportunity to pay homage at a special place linked to one's faith – is multicultural. Many Christians still routinely make the trip to the Sanctuary of our Lady of Lourdes where young Bernadette Soubirous claimed to have seen apparitions of the Virgin Mary over 150 years ago. Muslims are expected to visit Mohammed's birthplace at Mecca at least once in their lifetime. Millions of Hindus travel annually to "Ganga Ma" or Mother Ganges to have the purifying waters wash their sins away and, in doing so, they re-enact the myth of the sons of Sagara who thus reached Heaven. And the Western Wall in Jerusalem is the ritual focus of Jews from around the world who go there to push their written prayers into the cracks between the stones.

For those who do not belong to any orthodox religion, sacred places are also destinations for pilgrimage. Such spots include Chichen Itza in the Yucatan Peninsula of Mexico, Stonehenge in England, the Giza Pyramids of Egypt and Ayer's Rock in Australia's Northern Territories.

There are many ways in which walking a labyrinth and going on a pilgrimage are one and the same. Both can involve public and private states, being simultaneously individual and community experiences. As often happens during a group retreat, there is an overwhelming desire, at some point in a pilgrimage, to wish to abstain from superficial conversations and to separate yourself physically and spiritually from everyone else. This often signals a time when something of spiritual significance is about to happen and it is reminiscent of the calm and solitude many women seek before giving birth, particularly for the first time.

As with going on a pilgrimage, walking a labyrinth can be a life-changing adventure. That is not to say every walk is a "Road to Damascus experience" because the results are frequently much more subtle. Here are two stories as examples, the first from my own experience of the labyrinth.

LESSONS FROM THE LABYRINTH (I)

Liz's Story

I have always been someone for whom success has meant achieving specific goals rather than my taking any pleasure in the journey I made to get there. As often happens, this particular "thinking distortion" was not evident to me – until one occasion when I was walking the labyrinth outside the California Pacific Medical Center in San Francisco, an elegant Chartres design painted on concrete by Victoria Stone.

The irony is that I had walked Chartres-style labyrinths many times before, yet this was the first time I had this particular insight. If you have walked this design yourself, or if you trace your finger along the labyrinth (*see* page 113), you will know that within moments of entering the first pathway you come right to the edge of the center. You are so close to your goal but then find yourself being led away. And then again, within a relatively short amount of time you find yourself on the other side of the labyrinth, where the path again nudges the center, but it still does not lead directly to it. Then comes the real test of endurance when subsequent pathways lead you in a winding route further away from the goal.

As I walked this particular labyrinth I realized that at the start of projects I tended to be overconfident that I would reach my goal quickly and easily. Then, when something happened that denied me that result I became dispirited at the amount of time and effort I really need to apply – more than early signs seemed to suggest.

Now when such unrealistic thoughts come, I remind myself of the labyrinth and the circuitous route that must be taken to reach my goals rightfully at the appropriate time and in the appropriate way. And I focus on enjoying the journey I take to accomplish my projects, in the same way that I have trained myself to gain enormous pleasure from walking each of the labyrinth's pathways – not just in reaching the center.

Incidentally, as I sat making notes about this experience I looked up and saw a couple of pigeons fly down onto the labyrinth. At first I had the thought, "Wouldn't it be wonderful if they followed the pathways, just as I did?" But, of course, they didn't. As much as I have respect for the animal kingdom this brought home to me the fact that only we humans have the intelligence to consciously choose the path we are on. We can make choices about how we walk the labyrinth in the same way that we make choices about how we experience life.

Carole's Story

Carole wanted to work through certain career issues. Despite being one of the longest-serving members of her department, she had been passed over for promotion several times. She had never asked why, always telling herself that the other person was "better" or more deserving than she was – better educated, better connected or better liked.

The only day that week that Carole could spare the time to walk the labyrinth was on a Sunday afternoon. To her dismay she found that there was a group holding a ceremony there – which meant masses of people with the same idea. Carole called me and asked if she should postpone her walk until it was quieter? No, I urged her, if this was the environment she was being offered, there must be a good reason why it was so crowded. I will let Carole tell the rest of the story:

"The area around the labyrinth was pandemonium. We were actually standing in line waiting to enter and, because I'd hung back not wishing to break into the group, it took me a good half hour before I took my first, tentative steps.

"I don't know what I was expecting, but any pleasure I'd hoped to get from the experience was marred by all the stopping and starting. However, it wasn't until I'd meditated in the center for a short while and began to make my way out that I realized why the walk was

taking me so long and why I couldn't really get into it. I automatically stopped to let others pass me on the pathways; I put their needs before my own. Out of the corner of my eyes I could see one woman dressed in a bright red sweater and I was drawn to watch her. Every time she came face to face with a fellow walker she smiled, bowed slightly with her hands pressed together and moved respectfully forward as the other person stepped to one side. Not everyone accommodated her, but the majority did. She wasn't being aggressive, like some, just pleasantly assertive. Unfortunately, she had exited the labyrinth and was gone before I finished my walk so I never had a chance to talk with her.

"The realization didn't hit me straight away, but as I lay in bed the next morning it occurred to me that I was too accommodating at work. I never took the opportunity to let influential managers know what I had accomplished and I was letting less experienced co-workers sail right past me in the promotion stakes — just like the people on the labyrinth.

"That was a turning point for me. I was never going to advance my career if I kept holding back to suit other people. It's not the easiest thing in the world to change a long-held tendency and I certainly have no desire to turn into some megalomaniac bully, but I keep a picture of the Chartres labyrinth on my office wall to remind me that my journey is just as important as the next person's. I've also undergone assertiveness training to help me put my new belief into action."

Labyrinth Etiquette

Have you seen those notices on buses and subway trains which state that certain seats are to be given up for the elderly or people with disabilities? It is a sad reflection on society that we need to be reminded to give up our seat to someone with more pressing physical needs. In the same way, one would think that by knowingly undertaking a spiritual exercise it should not be necessary to worry over labyrinth etiquette. Yet many people do.

As caring, mutually dependent and connected souls sharing this planet it would be wonderful to think that all labyrinth walkers — indeed all people, whatever the environment they find themselves in — would be respectful and thoughtful towards others sharing that space. This is normally the case and there are mutually acceptable ways to pass fellow walkers even when the pathways are narrow or there are more people than usual traversing the labyrinth. Occasionally people "tut" or grumble under their breath when someone in front of them is not moving as fast they would like, but this is unnecessary and selfish.

However, since walking the labyrinth invariably teaches you something about yourself and how you negotiate life, prompting insights about how you might change your attitudes and behavior any time you choose, then all experiences in the labyrinth are beneficial. "Do as you would be done by" seems as good a maxim as any to follow when taking part in a labyrinth walk. If this remains a problem for you, then try and find a time when you can walk a labyrinth all by yourself.

DRAWING A LABYRINTH

Now it is time for you to experience the labyrinth for yourself, and discover ways in which you can integrate the labyrinth's lessons into your life today, even if there are no examples nearby for you to walk. To begin with, you will need to know how to draw one.

The Classical Seven-circuit Labyrinth

The labyrinth is a gloriously multi-faceted symbol. Viewed from an aerial perspective it reveals a single, inevitable route to a central goal or destination. Were walls to be constructed instead of open pathways, a labyrinth would seem a scary and confusing place. (This is another labyrinth "life message" about not building unnecessary defenses around yourself.) When looking at a drawing of a Classical seven-circuit labyrinth it may seem very complex. But when broken down into discrete stages, drawing labyrinths becomes a simple and enjoyable exercise that anyone can do.

Beginning with the "seed labyrinth" or basic form, drawing a Classical seven-circuit labyrinth is as straightforward as a "join-the-dots" game. Illustrations 1–9 take you through it step by step.

a)   *Begin by copying the basic form (1) which is simply a cross into which quarter are inserted four L-shapes with a dot in each corner. Make sure you have got this exactly right before moving onto the next step.*

Drawing a seven-circuit labyrinth.

b)   *Place your pencil (or pen – but it is easier to use a pencil so you can erase any mistakes) at the top of the cross and connect it in a curve to the next line end to create a hoop (2).*

c)   *Then place your pencil to the left of the first hoop and, again producing a curve, join it up to the top right-hand corner dot (3).*

d)   *The process continues in exactly the same way, always moving from the next left line end or dot, drawing curves that connect with the next line end or dot on the right (4–8).*

e)   *You should end up with the final line completing the labyrinth on the lowest end of the vertical line of the cross (9).*

This basic pattern can be adapted to all sizes of labyrinth. When wishing to draw an eleven-circuit labyrinth, for example, you simply need to start with an extra set of L-shapes within the basic form – you need the cross, the four L-shapes of the seven-circuit design plus an extra set of smaller Ls facing in the same direction before putting in the corner dots. For a fifteen-circuit labyrinth there are three such sets of L-shapes in each quadrant, then the dots. And, if you want to pare down to a three-circuit drawing, you simply omit the L-shapes altogether so you start with a cross and four dots in the open corners.

Your first attempts at drawing labyrinths may be a little wobbly. Practice makes perfect! The key thing is to enjoy doodling labyrinths. Once you have mastered this technique you will find it serves as an excellent light meditation and relaxation tool in itself. There are also other ways in which you can include labyrinth drawing into your life and it is up to you to use the labyrinth symbol in your own way, to best serve your unique needs. Below I set out several suggestions as to how you might use labyrinths to help you harness the self-healing power of your chakras.

THE LABYRINTH AND THE CHAKRAS

The seven pathways of the labyrinth you have drawn are neatly linked to the seven "chakras" or energy centers that are the basis of an ancient Hindu Ayurvedic system of healing.

Although the chakras relate to our subtle energy system (also known as the Universal Life Force) each of the seven major chakras are linked to our body's endocrine system and major organs. This approach to health is based on an understanding that we experience physical disease when there is a related blockage in the subtle energy system.

The best way of maintaining optimal mental and physical health, according to this philosophy, is to ensure that the chakras are balanced. Like seven cogs or wheels in a multi-connected system, the energy passing through the chakra system must be smooth and harmonious.

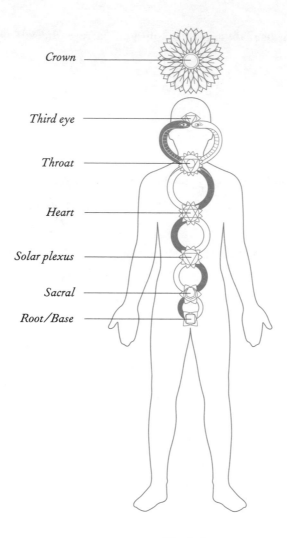

Crown

Third eye

Throat

Heart

Solar plexus

Sacral

Root/Base

The chakras.

PATHWAY	CHAKRA	COLOR	GLAND	BODY PART	LIFE TOPIC
1	Root/Base	Red	Adrenals	Bones, Skeleton	Survival/ Health
2	Sacral	Orange	Ovaries Testes	Sex organs, Bladder, Prostate	Emotional balance, Sexuality
3	Solar Plexus	Yellow	Pancreas	Digestive System, Muscles	Personal power, Self-will
4	Heart	Green	Thymus	Heart and Chest, Lungs, Circulation	Love and Relationships
5	Throat	Blue	Thyroid, Parathyroid	Mouth, Throat, Ears	Self-expression, Communication
6	Third eye	Indigo	Pituitary	Eyes, Base of Skull	Intuition, Inner Wisdom
7	Crown	Violet, Gold	Pineal	Cerebral cortex, Skin	Spirituality, Self-actualization

Working with the Chakras

There are a number of ways in which you can integrate chakra work and the labyrinth symbol, and with time you will develop your own strategies. The following are two favorite exercises of mine – one for physical problems and the other as a creative problem-solving exercise. For both, you need to number the seven pathways of a labyrinth. You may find it helpful to color them the color of each chakra.

Helping physical problems

Dysfunction in the chakra system, through blockages or the subtle energy moving too fast or too slowly, takes place before symptoms manifest themselves. You may wish to give yourself a chakra check each week or month to pre-empt future possible health problems. For this you will need a drawing of the seven-circuit labyrinth, numbered and/or colored appropriately, at least twenty minutes of quiet time when you can be by yourself, and in a warm, comfortable place where you will not be disturbed.

Begin by taking several slow, deep breaths and quietening your mind of distracting thoughts or concerns. Focus your gaze on your labyrinth and, moving through the pathways one by one, con-centrate on the associated body part. Ask your intuition for guidance as to how well the relevant chakra is functioning. I like to imagine a lotus flower, opening and closing like a self-regulating valve, to get some sense of how that part of my chakra system is performing.

Whenever you sense that part of your subtle energy system is unbalanced in any way, take time to meditate on what changes to your lifestyle or what medical intervention might be appropriate. Reading more about chakra correspondences will help you further.

Creative problem-solving

Problems often occur because we have not come to grips with all the factors affecting a particular issue – such as taking a new job without considering how the long traveling time will affect you. As you can see from the chart (*see* page 107), each labyrinth pathway and chakra corresponds to a different life topic. These can be used to anticipate a wide range of questions about whether a particular course of action is suitable for you. Here is the story of how using this technique worked for Shonah.

What should I do?

Shonah's dilemma was whether she should leave her job, friends, and family on the US west coast to join her boyfriend while he took an M.B.A. course in Boston. Shonah took as much time as she needed on each life topic, asking her intuition for guidance. The center of the labyrinth is open and uncolored, representing pure potential. If Shona's inner self presented no immediate solution by the time she reached the center of the labyrinth, she knew that this was not the appropriate time to make the right choice. Shonah's question was:

"Should I move to Boston with Josh for the next few years or stay in California with my friends, family and work and maintain the relationship from here?"

Here is how each of the seven labyrinth pathways and associated chakras were linked to questions that Shona needed to ask herself.

LIFE TOPIC	CHALLENGES TO THINK ABOUT
Health and security	How easy will it be for me to settle in a different part of the country; how will this affect me psychologically?
Emotional balance	Will a long-distance relationship fulfill us both? Can I trust Josh – and myself?
Personal power	How easy will it be for me to find a suitable job on the east coast?
Love and relationships	Do I love this man enough to sacrifice my current lifestyle?
Communication	Why have I resisted talking to Josh about how this decision is affecting me? Do we have communication issues neither of us is addressing?
Inner wisdom	Since this does not need to be an immediate yes/no decision – what other solutions should I be considering?
Spirituality	I've always believed that no choice is ever the wrong choice. Am I prepared to embrace that attitude for such a big decision as this one?

In addition to observing her thoughts, Shonah was sensitive to any bodily sensations associated with the chakras. When questioning herself about her job prospects on the east coast, Shonah experienced an excited fluttering in her solar plexus region (chakra pathway three) and realized that she had been dissatisfied at her current place of work for some time. She was, in fact, excited at the prospect of looking for a new job, irrespective of whether that was locally or on the other side of the United States.

After further deliberation, Shonah spoke to Josh at length and they agreed he should move to Boston alone with each of them taking turns to visit the other once a month. In that way Shonah could get a feel for the area and explore different employment prospects before selling up in California.

Creative visualization

There are many other topics to which each of the pathways of the seven-circuit labyrinth can be applied. One method I have developed is using the labyrinth as an eight-step creative visualization exercise in which you imagine you are walking a Cretan labyrinth and, as you move from one pathway to another, you focus on specific issues, as outlined below. The eighth pathway is represented by the center on the labyrinth.

PATHWAY	FOCUS	SELF-EXPLORATION
1	Vision	What compelling vision do you have for your life? What changes could you make to achieve balance among life areas including work/career, partnership, friends/social life, and health.
2	Tension	What are the key differences between what you have now and your dream life. What prevents you from achieving the latter?
3	Detail	How many steps or objectives will it take to reach your goals given that it is rarely possible to go from A to Z in one single step.
4	Change	Taking one task related to each of your objectives, what changes do you need to make to your attitude, behavior, or situation that will bring your vision closer to reality? Then commit to doing them.
5	Intuition	Why are you procrastinating? Does your dream vision come from your head or your heart? Does the answer to this offer you a clue?
6	Diversity	Who could you seek out to help you on your quest for success? What alternative viewpoint(s) would be of value to you in your mission? Seek them out.
7	The Unknown	Are you impeding your own success by being such a perfectionist that you are failing to move forward? Stop *doing* so much and learn how to *be*.
8	Destiny	Imagine a magic pool at the center of your mental labyrinth. Reach down to retrieve a symbolic gift from your Higher Self. Ask your intuition for help to discover what this symbol means. If you do not see an immediate connection with your situation, the meaning will unfold in the coming days or weeks.

If you are uncertain of how the pathways lead on from one to the other, use your paper labyrinth as a guide. As with any work of this nature, the key thing is to achieve a deep sense of relaxation, such as occurs just before sleep and waking, when creative connections are more likely to occur to you.

Making a Labyrinth Symbol

When using the labyrinth symbol as a focus for meditation or for tracing your finger along the pathways as a relaxation exercise, there is no need to confine yourself to paper. Many artistic types (and some who thought they never could be!) have found attractive large, flat pebbles, pieces of stone or wood and painted a Classical seven-circuit labyrinth on them. You could also use pieces of plastic, colored stickers or some other durable material to produce a mosaic or labyrinth collage that you could hang in your workplace or sacred space. Or buy or construct a shallow, square box, half fill it with sand and draw the labyrinth in that.

The materials that you use to create your own labyrinth, and the uses to which it can be put, are bounded only by the limits of your imagination. In Chapter 6, we look at how community groups have created their own labyrinths, and the uses to which they have put them.

A finger labyrinth.

chapter 5
LIVING LABYRINTHS

Life — Be in it.

AUSTRALIAN ADVERTISING SLOGAN, 1980S

BUILDING A LABYRINTH

*H*ere is where we put aside the theory and explore how ordinary individuals are bringing the labyrinth symbol to life in their lives and that of their communities. The simplest labyrinth design to reproduce is the Cretan or Classical version.

The Classical Seven-circuit Labyrinth

The number and width of your pathways and the amount of space you allow in the center is dependent on how much total space you have to work in. When constructing a seven-circuit labyrinth, the overall diameter is the sum of the width of 14 circuits plus the width of the center. All of these dimensions also have to be considered in the context of who will be using the labyrinth. Both wheelchairs and large animals – such as horses – require extra pathway space (*see* the story about Calvin Vanderhoof's and Joyce Leake's labyrinths, pages 125 and 136). And, if you plan to hold communal ceremonies in the center of your labyrinth or are laying it out for use by young schoolchildren, you may want to have normal sized pathways but a particularly wide center.

Traditionally, the center width is the same as that of the pathways for this design, however, many labyrinth walkers appreciate more space so several people can meditate there at the same time without feeling cramped. If you plan to make your pathways 2ft wide, your center could be twice that so the space the labyrinth would take up is calculated as follows:

$$14 \text{ pathways} \times 2 = 28\text{ft} + 4\text{ft for the center} = 32\text{ft total diameter}$$

Using that formula, having 3ft pathways in a seven-circuit design means a 48ft diameter ($14 \times 3 + 6 = 48$). If your space is limited, you have the option of reducing the number of circuits to five or even three. It is always best to start with the total width of space available and work backwards from there. Indeed, rather than trying to produce a seven-circuit labyrinth within a small garden space where the pathways would be so narrow that it would be like trying to walk a tightrope, I would suggest you reduce the number of circuits instead. Also, there is no reason why you should stick rigidly to a circular shape – particularly if your garden is oddly shaped. There are many fine examples of unusually structured labyrinths that are both fun and highly accessible for small spaces. These include a wonderful oblong shaped three-circuit labyrinth, popularly promoted by horticultural writers in the eighteenth century, as well as five-circuit circular and triangular ones illustrated in the *Architectura curiosa nova* written in 1664.

It is possible to incorporate a labyrinth into any space, even a window box – not to walk, but to have as an aide-mémoire to remind you to incorporate spiritual or self-development rituals in your everyday life.

The last time I visited my local art shop I came across bags of colored mosaics to use to make a variety of patterned objects, including a labyrinth. You could also collect crystal tumblestones (inexpensive pebbles of crystal that come in different various colors and shapes) and create a Cretan labyrinth design using those – even in a small garden. I am particularly drawn to Japanese-style gardens and think it would be fun to fill a shallow box with fine sand and lay a pebble or obsidian tumblestone labyrinth on that base. You are only limited by your own imagination. The labyrinth symbol is available to us all.

There are many different methods you can use to mark out the basic design. Some people follow the instructions for drawing a Cretan labyrinth (*see* page 115) and use a long wooden ruler or measuring stick to determine the width of the pathways. Others insert a stick in the exact center of their proposed labyrinth to which they tie a string to mark out semi-circles that form the top half of the labyrinth. The lower pattern is then extended around, with the final consideration being whether you want the entrance to be at the left or right of the center.

Labyrinth builders have employed many different materials and techniques to produce temporary lines, depending on whether the design is on grass, concrete, asphalt, or whatever. These include flour, chalk, small pebbles, surveyors' flags, and digging small trenches. Your choice will depend on your environment and social circumstances. If you live in a wet area and can only work on the labyrinth intermittently, you will need to use something more enduring than flour or chalk.

You can always practice laying a temporary seven-circuit labyrinth in a local community hall by using masking tape or rope. (Check first whether the tape you use is likely to leave a mark on the flooring.) Aside from that, bear in mind that the Cretan design is much simpler and can look as effective as the more elaborate Chartres-style labyrinth – plus you can have fun painting each pathway with the colors of the rainbow or laying crystals or obsidian (volcanic glass) or even tiny mosaics around the edges.

Whatever you decide, always have a drawing to follow while you are constructing the labyrinth, to make sure you are laying it out properly.

The Eleven-pathway Chartres Design

The Chartres design is a little more involved, but if you plan it out on paper first and understand the proportions and how everything fits together then you will not go far wrong.

Alternative labyrinth patterns.

Again, start by considering how much space you have available, including taking into account an area around the labyrinth where people can sit or stand while waiting to walk it themselves. The size of this area will depend on how busy you expect the labyrinth to get – a little "market research" beforehand might be a good idea. When you have a relatively small space you may want to consider reducing the number of pathways rather than making them too narrow. Anything less than 18 inches makes it difficult for people to pass each other, although this is not necessarily a bad thing and can act as the catalyst for some valuable insights.

A standard Chartres-style labyrinth comprises eleven pathways plus the perimeter – that is, you will need to draw twelve concentric circles. The center accounts for a quarter of the total diameter.

Working backwards for this example: assume a total space of 50ft square in which you want to incorporate space for a few benches or a garden border. You have decided to make your labyrinth 44ft wide, in order to leave 3ft around it (which will be reduced slightly by the lunations, *see* page 45). Dividing 44ft by 4 gives us the width of the center – in this case, 11ft, with the remaining 33ft to be divided by 22 (the total number of circuits). Hence each pathway becomes 1½ft wide.

As with the Cretan labyrinth, you can use a stick and string to determine where to mark each of the concentric circles. Just remember that, for the center (the best place to start), the length of the string is equal to the radius (half the diameter) and in the case of our example is 5½ft.

I have heard of two other, ingenious ways of marking out the concentric circles (these techniques also apply to producing the top half of the Cretan design). When preparing the ground for the construction of the first labyrinth at the Museum of International Folk Art in Santa Fe, New Mexico, one of the team produced a clever wooden gadget, rather like a giant compass made up of 12 pieces of board screwed together which, when opened out, revealed a screw jutting out of each piece at the exact place where the lines were to be marked. When this was dragged across the sandy base it scratched out all twelve concentric circles simultaneously.

Marge McCarthy (*see* page 133) makes Chartres-style labyrinths using a length of string which will extend to the intended outer perimeter, along which are knots at the appropriate distances for each of the pathways. The string is then stretched out and a team of people places a small stone in line with the knot, whereupon the string is moved around a little further and another stone placed accordingly. This is a simple and very effective way of starting to build a stone labyrinth, particularly when you have lots of eager helpers.

It is essential you work with an actual drawing of the Chartres labyrinth if you are planning to duplicate it (the "real thing" being 40ft in diameter). However, be creative! Take a look at some of the newer labyrinth designs and do not be afraid either to copy one that resonates with your group or produce a style of your own.

One way to personalize a basic labyrinth design is to have something special in the center. Aside from large boulders or small trees and bushes, ideas could include a sundial, a layout of crystals or

The Chartres labyrinth.

tumblestones that can be reconfigured at whim, large plastic play bricks, a meditation stool or a small sand pit as a canvas for your creative expression. You are only bounded by your own imagination – let it run wild!

LABYRINTHS IN THE COMMUNITY

What might a prison, a hospital, a bed and breakfast, and a garden in memory of war veterans have in common? Or a church, a retreat, and a high school for that matter? You will not be surprised to learn that each of these seemingly disparate communities have benefited from establishing local labyrinths.

Few, if any, of us journey through life totally alone. We are influenced, shaped, developed, and strengthened by our relationships with others. Some of the most valuable lessons around the nature of love, sacrifice, betrayal, and neglect come from our intimate relations with others. Most often it is only possible to accept, face up to and overcome inappropriate attitudes, beliefs, and behaviors in ourselves when we see them reflected in others. While a period of solitude is a wonderful way of developing a relationship with yourself, it is on the testing ground of interpersonal communication – be it with parents, siblings, friends or partners – that you discover whether the lessons you have learned from being alone are superficial or deeply ingrained.

The same is true of walking the labyrinth. It is both an individual and a community experience; one which offers valuable insights into how we interact with people at work, in our social life or just generally. Building a labyrinth, too, can be a wonderfully humbling, shared experience. I have chosen five inspiring examples to share with you in this chapter.

The value of these stories is manifold. They illustrate the many different environmental and social contexts in which building a community labyrinth can occur. In addition, each one contains useful tips on overcoming the challenges involved in designing and implementing the Cretan and Chartres designs. They are uplifting tales that demonstrate how anything can be achieved when you put your mind to it.

All of these examples come from the United States where rural dwellers have the space to indulge their passion for labyrinths. Some of the labyrinths mentioned here are up to 90ft in diameter. The aim is simply to demonstrate the creative uses to which labyrinths can be put and this may stimulate you to think about how you might integrate a labyrinth into your community. Remember, you do not need a huge amount of space in order to benefit from the labyrinth and its energy – just the patience to locate the right spot for your needs and the loving care with which each of the following individuals created theirs.

LESSONS FROM THE LABYRINTH (2)

Along a stretch of Highway 97 at the base of Mount Shasta in northern California, there is a sign alerting travelers to the Weed Living Memorial Sculpture Gardens. Within these gardens there is a black marble wall honoring local members of the armed services who took part in conflicts from World War I through to Vietnam. At one time, the main attractions here were the huge metal sculptures depicting various war themes to be discovered among the 58,000 trees planted in memory of all those who died in the Vietnam War. Today, people also come from far and wide to walk the Living Memorial labyrinth – a project conceived, lobbied for, and brought to fruition by a local woman, Calvin Vanderhoof.

Remembrance and Healing

Calvin, an HIV/Aids outreach worker, was first introduced to the labyrinth symbol at a conference she attended several years ago. Every morning during that week Calvin walked the labyrinth and found that it had a calming effect on her. In her words, the passion to continue the ritual "just took hold" and by the time she left the conference she was wondering how she could introduce a labyrinth to her home town of Weed. The nearby Living Memorial Gardens seemed the obvious location, particularly as it was already designated as a place of remembrance and healing.

While everyone thought she had gone mad, and the local foundation which maintained the land were concerned about the sort of strange people who might want to walk a labyrinth, Calvin remained focused, determined and sure of success. Having gathered a vast amount of information about labyrinths and the different ways of constructing them, she took the advice of a local contractor and settled on red and black stone pavers – the material used by many local authorities to pave public places. Calvin had roughly costed out the project and she applied for, and received, $12,000 from the McConnell Foundation which distributes grants for community projects across the region. She also got in touch with a craftsman who made wooden finger labyrinths and raffled or sold these to raise extra funds.

Two years after having first thought of, "Wouldn't it be great to have a local labyrinth?" Calvin's dream came true. Her husband, Dale, had modified the Chartres labyrinth, producing a design for a much simpler, five-circuit layout. Calvin hired a local construction company to prepare the area, clearing away bushes and laying a fine, gravel base which, when wet, has the properties of cement.

Knowing that she wanted an entrance to the east, just beyond the Memorial Gardens' car park, Dale secured a stake at what would be the exact center of the labyrinth and extended four lengths of string to the proposed outer edge in each direction – north, south, east, and west. Then, using a 5ft length of string attached to the center stake, Dale described a circle 10ft in diameter. Section by section of this circle (and, subsequently, the rest of the labyrinth) was covered with 1 inch-deep builders' sand with the red-brown pavers laid in rows on top. It took the four-person team a day to get this far. The outer pavers were then cut to fit the circle exactly and edged with a row of black ones.

Next, they laid the straight, east-facing pathways that would lead in and out of the labyrinth with red pavers, again separating and edging them with black ones. Each pathway was to be 30 inches wide – big enough to accommodate a wheelchair for any disabled veterans who wished to navigate the labyrinth. Once this had been accomplished, each of the five circular pathways was added, radiating out from the center. Finally, the circumference of the Living Memorial labyrinth was edged by black pavers and, beyond that, an 18 inch-wide moat of gravel.

Pavers are made with little notches on their side edges which allow for a slight gap between them when placed in a row. Once the 39ft-wide labyrinth had been completed, more builders' sand was flooded over the top of the design, some of which settled in the gaps. The excess was swept off. Finally, the pavers were sprayed with a sealer to protect them from frost and snow and to make it easier to wash off any graffiti.

The final result is a very beautiful, simple labyrinth in an area of outstanding scenic beauty where the magnificent 14,000ft high snow-capped Mount Shasta rises majestically to the east. It cost approximately $13,000 to complete, with local firms donating materials such as gravel and sand and many individuals making donations. Other companies offered discounts so the team could buy a picnic table and benches for visitors to rest awhile.

In an area with many trees and the chance of roots pushing up through the ground, pavers are a particularly practical material. If one becomes dislodged or damaged it can be lifted up and replaced without affecting the rest of the design.

The labyrinth team incorporated nice little touches such as marking one of the outside black pavers with an arrow and the letter "N" to indicate North. Sometimes people leave money in the center of the labyrinth to help with the cost of maintenance – others, gifts of gratitude or remembrance such as flowers.

Calvin Vanderhoof says that people come day and night, summer, and winter, to walk the Living Memorial Sculpture Garden. As the full moon rises over the nearby mountain the labyrinth becomes spotlighted in its glow. And, when there is 6 inches or less of snow on the surrounding ground the labyrinth remains clear and walkable – a remarkable sight made possible by the achievement of a remarkable person.

The following is a wonderfully inspiring, multi-faceted story of how the labyrinth symbol can contribute to education. It also outlines some of the challenges facing anybody who decides to paint a labyrinth on concrete.

My husband and I had printed out the Grace Cathedral labyrinth locator for northern California (*see* Resources, page 173) and, on a trip to Sonoma County, we stopped by San Andreas High School in the small town of Larkspur. There, in the middle of the basketball court, was a perfect example of a Chartres-style labyrinth painted on concrete. Joseph Rafalo, the math teacher responsible for this project takes up the story.

Educational Tool

"I've been a math teacher for 21 years and have always looked for hands-on ways to present the subject so that the kids understand that solving equations and suchlike has some meaning in the real world. When I first came across the labyrinth pattern from walking one with a friend, I realized right away that it would fit right into a lesson on geometry. Little did I realize then just how many invaluable lessons — other than just in mathematics — that the introduction of that beautiful symbol would bring.

"Let me give you a little bit of background about this High School to put this story in some kind of perspective. It's what's called a 'continuation' or 'alternative' school and by State

law every school district has to have one. There are many reasons why kids come here. Some have behavioral difficulties and have been thrown out of other schools — many for attendance or drug-related problems. Some just didn't fit in with the mainstream school system because they don't get on so well with regimentation and need to go to a smaller, more personal educational establishment like ours. I'd say the majority of teenagers who come here have had a lot of problems at other schools, while others have just opted for an alternative approach to their education. The classes are smaller which means they get much more individual attention.

"One of the girls in my class four years ago had come to San Andreas High School for the latter reason. She was very artistic and extremely good in the math class. When I showed the group a drawing of the labyrinth they all thought it was really cool, so I challenged them to draw it. Being the Chartres design, which is fairly complicated, this was a much harder task than drawing the Classical seven-circuit labyrinth. This young girl did a wonderful job of drawing this intricate design and since she'd enjoyed it so much I asked her to head a project in which we'd paint our own labyrinth on the basketball court.

"The school principal at the time was a former math teacher who took the attitude that whatever his staff wanted to do to bring lessons alive for the students, he would back one hundred per cent. If I thought that this was a worthwhile project, then that was good enough for him. All I needed was the okay from the rest of the teaching staff, particularly since we would be taking over the basketball court — which is situated right in the middle of

the school buildings — for some time. Actually, we didn't realize just how long a time. This turned out to be a much more time consuming and challenging project than I originally envisioned.

"The first hurdle was how to draw perfect circles. I'd heard from a friend of mine who constructs wooden floors and has worked on school gymnasia that there's a machine you can use to mark out the circles for basketball courts. He was going to loan one to us but then found he couldn't get permission to do so. By this time the class was all hyped up, so we went back to acting like ancient Greeks — with stick and rope. With one pupil standing in the middle holding tightly onto a stick, from which was attached a length of string and a piece of chalk, we drew circle after concentric circle on the concrete. Using chalk meant that if we didn't get it right first time (and that was the case more often than not) we could erase the line and start again. This took weeks rather than days and luckily we live in California so we didn't have to worry about the rain erasing our work.

"Once we had the right number of concentric circles drawn we then had to convert them into pathways by closing up the appropriate ends with semi-circles. We first measured the intended width of each pathway and then made a cardboard template that would fit inside and cut that into a semi-circle. That's how we drew the turns.

"At last we were ready to paint — but that, too, proved more difficult than we'd thought because ordinary paint wears off concrete too easily — especially with teenagers trampling* across it every day. So, after some research, we ended up getting in touch with the Highways Department to find out what they used to paint lines on roads. It's not easy to get this stuff and we had to buy it in huge quantities and have still got gallons of leftover paint stored somewhere.

"My main concern was that we'd end up making a real mess and not be able to wash it off, but the kids were painstaking in the care they took. It was wonderful to watch students who normally can't wait to escape when they hear the school bell, stay long after they needed to, just to work on the labyrinth.

"Ironically — and I advise anyone not to trust to blind faith — we hadn't walked the labyrinth while we still only had the chalk lines. But the student in charge of the project guaranteed it would be perfect — and it is. People still come here from miles around to walk our labyrinth, which is in a beautiful setting at the base of Mount Tam.

"What did the students learn from this exercise? On the math side they experienced geometry in action, learning about the different degrees and angles and how geometry could be used in everyday life to construct circles. But they learned much more besides. This was a memorable experience of teamwork and the logical progression of thought from the inception of an idea through to what is required to carry it out. We all learned how to apply our creativity to overcome obstacles and that when you're really passionate and focused, anything is possible."

This seems an appropriate point to mention the different ways in which introducing labyrinths to younger children is of emotional and spiritual value to them. Marge McCarthy is a retired school psychologist in Santa Fe, New Mexico who decided to combine her love of children with her passion for labyrinths. Marge was instrumental in getting a labyrinth built outside the Museum of International Folk Art in Santa Fe (*see* page 121 and below). She now helps organize the building of labyrinths in elementary schools in her area, for children aged between 5 and 12 years, generally going in to talk with them beforehand about how they can be used.

Children

On one occasion a group of children had already been walking their community labyrinth for part of the school year, which is how Marge was able to tell me this story.

"When I went around the room asking the children how they had used the labyrinth, one six-year old girl told the group how she had thought about 'Mommy Temple.' When another child asked, 'Who's that?' the girl replied – although in much simpler terms – that it was her birth mother.

"The teacher decided to intervene at this point and said that the little girl didn't have to talk about this if she didn't want to. But the child wanted to share with her classmates – a group of 30 children all sitting in a circle – that her mother had died giving birth to her and she was being raised by her grandparents who had adopted her. This was the

first time that little girl had disclosed to the other children that she was not living with her birth mother.

"This, to me, is an example of the way the labyrinth acts as a catalyst, offering us the security to speak our truth, to go inside and get in touch with things that are bothering us — even when you're a six-year-old child."

A second poignant example of the way the labyrinth can help children express their feelings in a safe and healthy way came about when Marge encouraged a group of elementary school children to stand around the labyrinth perimeter, holding hands. One by one they entered the labyrinth, with no one uttering a sound until they had all completed their walk and returned to the class-room. Marge invited them to talk about their experiences. One 7-year-old boy mentioned that his dog had died a couple of weeks earlier and that he hadn't been able to cope with it. But after walking the labyrinth he realized that his dog would live in his heart forever.

Here is just a small selection of the quotes Marge has taken the time to record, demonstrating more of the benefits of labyrinths for today's youngsters — and their teachers who are always looking for effective ways to calm children down so they can study better.

"I decided to feel better about doing my homework. I thought about the reasons why I feel bad when I don't do it and all the ways I try to get out of it. It gets me nowhere. I just feel worse. I thought about how the people feel who have to deal with me."

"I thought about a problem I have. My Mom is getting a cat. I have a bird and a fish and I am worried about the situation. But I am no longer worried (after walking the labyrinth) because I realized that my dog will chase the cat and my bird and fish will be safe."

"I figured out a way to talk to people to get their attention. It is better to talk than to grab someone's neck when they are bugging you. I will just insist that we talk."

"I thought about my biggest dream. I want to be a singer and I want my family to understand how serious I am."

"I decided to go home tonight and say sorry to my sister."

And, sometimes it is just enough to do this:

"I thought of nothing but the sun on my back."

It was thanks to her beloved horse, Riley, that Joyce Leake developed her innate talent for animal communication, working with animals and their human caregivers to help enhance their relationship. When he died, this prompted Joyce to create a wonderful labyrinth memorial dedicated – not just to Riley – but to all the animal friends that other people have lost.

Animal Remembrance

Joyce has always had an empathy with horses, so who better – her husband thought – to pour TLC on Riley, a sad, ill and wasted character he had found, who had been ridden too hard, too young. The moment she saw him, Joyce fell in love with Riley and slowly and gently nursed him back to health – certainly well enough that he could be taken out for light rides. Unfortunately, Riley died some time afterwards, which was devastating for Joyce. At that time she was only casually interested in labyrinths, having been introduced to the concept by an artist friend who had built one in the nearby town of Elizabeth, Colorado. However, after Riley's death an idea began to form in Joyce's mind and she decided to build one on her own 60-acre property – close to where Riley was buried.

Joyce gathered together a group of around 40 volunteers who arranged the rocks that her husband, Roy, brought in from the construction sites he worked on. But before putting these friends to work, Joyce, her husband and a third helper marked out the land using the traditional stick and rope technique – with Joyce being the one who got to stand in the middle holding the end of the rope while the other two used the stick as a tracing device onto which lime was spread. (The best kind is the lime used to mark out lawn tennis courts, or cricket and baseball pitches.) The day after, the volunteers arrived and chose the rocks, which they laid over the lime tracing.

Joyce's Cretan-style labyrinth is 90ft in diameter, that being a much simpler pattern to follow when accompanied by a large animal, and has pathways that are 5ft wide – big enough to walk or ride a horse through. Dogs, cats, guinea pigs, llamas, and alpacas are just some of the creatures that have walked the labyrinth with their owners. Joyce's corgis, particularly, loved to plant themselves within the design and animal lovers can sit on a large rock in the center of the labyrinth or on the wooden chairs on the west side, watching the long grass softly sway in the Colorado wind like wheat.

What makes this labyrinth particularly special is that Joyce's labyrinth is a place where people can honor their dead animals in a unique and interactive way. She provides visitors with paint and brushes so they can write the names on the rocks of any animals they have loved that have passed away. The whole idea is very fluid. People are allowed to bring their own rocks to add to the labyrinth and they can place personal items underneath them – like a lock of hair or favorite toy – to remind them of their dead pet. Joyce says that the painted names fade away after about a year and she believes this is how it should be.

The labyrinth provides both a memorial to animals that have had a profound effect on their owner's lives and a place where beings of all kinds can relax and just "be." Joyce recalls the visit by a working student of an internationally known horse trainer who brought with him a horse that was finding training to be a particularly difficult and stressful experience. Afterwards, Joyce asked the man what he had felt or hoped to feel while riding the horse through the labyrinth. To which he replied that it was simply a wonderful opportunity for the animal to just walk in peace and not have to "do" anything.

Joyce's labyrinth, built in a grass meadow with stones and boulders of all shapes and sizes outlining the pathways, is little trouble to maintain. She lives in an area of the United States that does not get a lot of rain, so she only has to mow it three times a year. The areas around the edges of the stones are kept tidy by using a Weedeater (known as a "strimmer" in the UK) and as long as visitors call in advance everyone is welcome to enjoy the labyrinth, accompanied by their animals, or alone – to remember and honor ones that they have lost.

More and more health farms, spas and retreats are incorporating labyrinths as a meditation amenity for their guests. This story, from the owners of the Star Hill Inn in Sapello, New Mexico – the US's only astronomical retreat – highlights what they needed to do to construct their mountain meadow labyrinth. Rae Ann Kumelos Mahon's story includes some valuable tips if you are thinking of marking out a labyrinth on grass.

Wild Meadow Labyrinth

"I had read a magazine article about labyrinths and was completely entranced by the idea – so much so that creating our own became my 40th birthday present. We ordered the information from Grace Cathedral and the more we looked into the concept of labyrinths the more fascinating the project became, particularly since sacred geometry links so well with astronomy, which is the focus of our retreat.

"The package we received contained a great deal of information about the labyrinth's origins – as far as anyone knows – but not as much as we could have used. Depending on the width of the pathways the diameter of the labyrinth varies enormously and we weren't sure how big we wanted the final design to be. The determining factor came from a surprising source – WalMart. That's where we bought the lawn mower that we use to differentiate between the walkways and the meadow in between. For this to work, the walking path has to be wide enough to mow. As it turned out, our labyrinth ended up being 90ft wide – luckily not a problem for us as Star Hill is situated on 200 acres.

"We chose the meadow as somewhere private and acceptable to our guests; it's a beautiful, open space with a terrific view in all four directions. But also because we had walked the land and that spot resonated with us the most – it's a very special place. Since marking it out, we've found that many of our animal friends migrate into the middle of the labyrinth – including a bear, elk, a bob cat, and a flock of wild turkeys.

"*Luckily, my husband Phil has a degree in mathematics, as laying the labyrinth out wasn't easy. We especially wanted the labyrinth to be aligned to the summer solstice sunrise, which is our wedding anniversary and for us the lightest, happiest day of the year. Phil worked on the computer to get the exact coordinates to identify the center of the labyrinth, which is where we placed the first stick, attached with string. While we'd originally thought we'd use cooking flour to mark the outline on the grass, we ended up using something more secure — surveyors' sticks with flags on. We then used black garden markers to differentiate the pathways before cutting them out using the push mower.*

"*In late summer it looks particularly beautiful with wild flowers and grasses growing between the walkways. All are natural to this region and represent the colors of New Mexico — lavender and amethyst, sage green and bright yellow. We've erected a latilla pole — a piece of aspen — facing the entrance to our labyrinth which has ribbons tied on it for each of the different chakra colors [see page 107], as well as wind chimes.*

"*Our guests love the labyrinth. Star Hill attracts a wide variety of people, many of whom are scientifically minded and have not heard of the labyrinth. They find it non-threatening because it's non-denominational and isn't connected to any particular religion or religious organization.*

"*We've been honored to have facilitated a lot of special experiences through the labyrinth. My favorite story is that of a male guest who had never walked a labyrinth before but was interested in trying ours. Once he got to the middle he'd had enough and didn't want to spend the time winding his way back out, so he began walking diagonally across the pathways straight to the perimeter. As he was doing so, he realized that this was a pattern in his life – he doesn't finish things. That was a real awakening for him. We're not saying 'Come to the labyrinth and experience an incredible epiphany', just enjoy the meditative aspects of it in a beautiful, natural setting."*

There is a further story connected to this labyrinth. One year Phil and Rae Ann discovered that their two 5,000 gallon water tanks were leaking, losing a precious resource that not only supplied their own home with water, but also all their guest houses. Traditional methods were unable to identify the source of the leak and the Mahons were told by contractors that they would probably have to dig up the whole half mile of pipe to find it. Phil decided to walk the labyrinth to see whether he could get a fresh perspective on what was, to them, a calamity. While he was doing so a picture of a gopher (a small, burrowing animal common to the region) came into his head.

Rae Ann, who is trained in animal communication and shamanic journeying, decided to contact spiritually the gophers living on the land and during this experience was given a mental picture of where the leak could be found. They discovered it right outside the entrance to the labyrinth, just where the gophers told her it would be. Although there is no rational explanation for it, some dowsers will

tell you that labyrinths attract water and you should never build them anywhere near an important water supply or it will run dry. This is why it is important to follow the guidelines on dowsing (*see* page 60) and, like the early designers and builders, take into account the importance of acknowledging and respecting the earth energy and harmony with nature that you want to tap into. These ancient energies penetrate the earth deeply and are thought to account for the many leaks that labyrinth owners – like the Mahons – have had to deal with.

FURTHER DESIGNS AND USES

I hope you have been inspired by these stories of "ordinary" people making an extraordinary contribution to their lives and that of their communities. Once you begin to delve into labyrinths more deeply, accessing websites and perhaps joining the mailing lists of labyrinth groups, you will discover even wider applications. For example, recent newsletters from Grace Cathedral in San Francisco – the birthplace of the contemporary labyrinth movement in the US – included stories of how walking the labyrinth was being of benefit to inmates in a male prison in Monterey, California and The Louisiana Correctional Institute for Women in St. Gabriel, Louisiana. In the latter case, the walk which took place on March 2001 involved 21 inmates, some serving life sentences, and an equal number of "Angel FreePeople" – women from all walks of life who interact with the prisoners, one-on-one.

In the Resources section (*see* page 172) you will find a list of organizations – principally in the US where there is a wider market for them – through whom it is possible to rent or buy canvas labyrinths. This is an option to consider, particularly if you are arranging a community event and want to introduce a labyrinth walk. But whether you design and build your own labyrinth or borrow one for a while, there is no end of applications to which you can put it.

As we have seen from the stories told in this chapter, labyrinths can have value for groups whose goals are either sacred or secular. They have found their way into a wide number of churches – Catholic, Methodist, Episcopalian, and Unitarian – as well as being established in universities, spas and health resorts, bed and breakfasts, health centers and hospitals. This reflects the need of people of all faiths and backgrounds for a means of meditating – with all the benefits that such regular practice brings – other than simply sitting and trying to clear one's mind. In this sense, walking a labyrinth is a more accessible and realistic way for them to "take time out," and is particularly appealing to those of us who find it difficult to sit still for any length of time.

Additionally, there is the beneficial ritual aspect of working with the labyrinth as a way of scheduling time when, just by placing one foot in front of another, we can engender a sense of continuity, groundedness and control with manifold therapeutic potential for us all. A canvas or permanently constructed labyrinth on the premises of many businesses would help employees reduce their stress levels and boost their creativity and sense of satisfaction.

As well as being a wonderful tool for establishing a sense of community among people, the labyrinth offers us the opportunity for some personal soul-searching, as we discovered our exploration of the hero's journey (*see* chapter 3). In the final chapter there are some more stories — this time of individuals whose lives have been changed profoundly through their exposure to labyrinths.

chapter 6

CHANGING THE WORLD, ONE PERSON AT A TIME

"The Constitution only gives people the right to pursue happiness. You have to catch it yourself."

BENJAMIN FRANKLIN, US STATESMAN, 1706–1790

Interacting with labyrinths is a very individual experience. There is no single way of negotiating labyrinths and the key thing is trust to your own intuition as to what is right for you. This is self-development at its most effective. Not by slavishly following the instructions of some "expert" or "guru," but by believing in your own unique connection to a Higher Power – that spiritual essence that lies within each one of us and which only needs to be heeded to direct us to a more deeply satisfying and joyful life. Different people react in different ways to exposure to the labyrinth and we can see from the stories that follow how the symbol has changed their lives – often quite dramatically. The Vietnamese Buddhist monk, Thich Nhat Hanh has written:

Walking meditation is meditation while walking. We walk slowly, in a relaxed way, keeping a tight smile on our lips. When we practice this way, we feel deeply at ease, and our steps are those of the most secure person on earth. All our sorrows and anxieties drop away, and peace and inner joy fill our hearts. Anyone can do it. It only takes a little time, a little mindfulness, and the wish to be happy.

This observation was echoed by one woman I spoke with after she had completed her walk of the Mizmaze on St. Catherine's Hill, Winchester, England:

"It slows me down, even though I'm the sort of person who is always rushing from one place to the next. It's quite weird the effect that walking these pathways has on me, as if time has taken on a different meaning and all that matters is what I'm doing right here, right now. I never really understood what was meant by 'living in the moment' until I began to walk the labyrinth. Its power, for me, is that I couldn't do otherwise. I just become hypnotized – changed – into this calm individual whom I hardly recognize from the woman I am outside. That's what appeals to me about the labyrinth – that it's a practical approach to this nebulous concept we call spirituality."

Here are some personal recollections of labyrinths and how they affect the very different individuals who have benefited from incorporating them into their lives.

LESSONS FROM THE LABYRINTH (3)

A "Spiritual Tuning Fork"

Nicholas Halpin is a counselor at Dundee University in Scotland where he is responsible for the Labyrinth tapestry, a 36ft diameter canvas replica of the Chartres labyrinth. A close friend and colleague, Andi Lothian, had been introduced to the labyrinth while at a workshop in the United States and he insisted that they bring the symbol to Dundee. The canvas labyrinth is occasionally set out in the University Chapel, a beautiful circular building presided over by a Hugh Lorimer sculpture – a truly inspiring setting where, surrounded by perfumed candles and graced by gentle music, the labyrinth has become a natural focus for prayer, meditation and reflection. As Nicholas explains:

"For me, the labyrinth is like a spiritual tuning fork – it creates a lot of energy. The more people who are walking it at one time, the more energy there is which is very tangible in terms of the warm, tingling feeling I get from it. And even when I come off the canvas and sit near it, I can feel the energy pulsating off the labyrinth in waves, a clear demonstration of spiritual energy.

"The thing I have learned is that in general people who walk the labyrinth do so to de-stress themselves. They probably lead very busy lives therefore deliberately walk in a

measured way in order to slow themselves down. But for someone like myself whose job requires me to stay calm – I run the counseling service at the University – then I find it more beneficial to walk the labyrinth rather quickly. Indeed, I've seen people literally pirouette around it and children like to run around it. The notion of walking very slowly is fine for lots of people but much depends on what you need to get out of it most. After all, a meditative state takes lots of different forms, according to different needs. By navigating the labyrinth in a fast way I find the experience frees me up – in particular, my creativity.

"I once walked a labyrinth at a rate of knots, having a meeting to attend in 20 minutes. I wheeled around it and came out with a complete poem in my head.

"The Dundee University labyrinth has gradually drawn a devoted following in the Tayside area and in the two years since we introduced it, several hundred people have learned to trust the gift of its energy and inspiration. Their comments, recorded at the end of their many walks, echo its peace and mystery. It's certainly been a truly formative experience for me, encouraging my spiritual journey and giving me the confidence to re-connect with the deeper elements of my life."

Learning Life's Lessons

Kimberley Anderson is a spa consultant and founder of Big Pond Marketing in San Francisco, California. Kim would normally meditate in the sacred space she has created in her home in order to find an answer to a question or problem that she is experiencing. But she agreed to try walking the labyrinth as it might be a valuable alternative, given that she was at a career crossroads in her life. Kim decided to hold the question of "Am I on the right path?" in her mind before entering the labyrinth, in the hope that walking this unicursal maze would alert her to which direction she should be taking in her life.

"I felt a little intimidated at first, particularly since there seemed to be 'experienced' walkers moving through the labyrinth and I didn't know what was proper etiquette. I had been assured that there was no wrong way to walk the labyrinth, so I accepted this, took off my shoes and waited a few moments before entering the path. I admit to feeling slightly disappointed as I walked through the pathways because I'd expected a flood of answers to come and to achieve instant enlightenment. But the experience was much subtler. As I made a mental note of the thoughts that were passing through my head, I noticed certain significances and realized that universal advice was indeed coming through.

"My first impression was of the warmth of the concrete beneath me, and feeling every inch of the soles of my feet. It reminded me of the carefree days of summer when I was a child and the feel of the hot pavement on my bare feet. It brought a wave of emotions, mainly sadness from the loss of those days and the immense pressures I was feeling as an adult trying to keep myself afloat as an independent business consultant. I was also keenly aware of my pace. I felt at first that I was going too fast, but then it was difficult to go slowly. I was very conscious of doing it 'right' and always comparing myself to the other people that were on the path who seemed far more experienced, and tried hard to be aware of them so as not to violate some sacred rule of conduct. I felt exhausted.

"Halfway in, it struck me that I wasn't sure how to come back out. Once I'd reached the center did I simply walk out across the labyrinth and ignore the path that had taken me in? As I watched the others I saw that once they had spent some time contemplating in the center, they simply turned around and took the same path out. There is no easy way in or out, there are no shortcuts and whatever you did to get you to where you are is what is needed to get you back out.

"So I started concentrating on the path in front of me and noticed that the concrete itself had a certain sparkle to it. Concrete is a really commonplace material, yet it contained a hidden beauty which I'd never observed before because I was always looking up ahead. In addition to the inherent glitter in the concrete, someone had thrown some sparkles on the ground. As I walked through them, some of the sparkles attached to my feet. To me, this

represented how we are touched by others who have traveled the path before us — and by our environment. Indeed, we take a little of our experiences and surroundings wherever we go.

"The 'Aha!s' that I got from walking the labyrinth that day were that I needed to go at my own pace and not worry about what others were doing around me. Each path is unique to the individual. There is no wrong or right way. How I walk my own path is wholly determined by me. I also learned that even the mundane can have sparkle and that when we focus on the present moment we can find joy.

"I suppose the answer to my question of whether I am on the right path was answered as I reflected on the labyrinth's twists and turns. My mind wandered occasionally, wondering where I was on the path and how far I had to go to get to the center. Just when I thought I was getting close, I would find that I was winding back to the perimeter of the labyrinth again. So I decided to stop worrying about where I was and just focus on the immediate path before me and the experiences that I was having along the way. Eventually, I realized, I will end up reaching my goal — as long as I keep moving forward."

Living with the Labyrinth

Julie Mitchell lives in Coarsegold, California, a small historic mining town that is a gateway to Yosemite National Park, around which Julie and her husband Michael love to explore the old communities along the 49-er trail. Julie describes herself as primarily a wife, mother, and grandma but she is also a student of herbal medicine, a Reiki Master and a mixed media artist. She has four children and three grandchildren, the eldest of whom lives nearby in Oakhurst, where her husband has a barber shop.

"My labyrinth story began about a year ago when I read a posting on the Internet from a woman who had discovered the healing powers of walking a labyrinth. I didn't know anything about labyrinths but the idea of a walking meditation sounded a good idea to me.

"I can't explain the pull the labyrinth had for me but I became obsessed with including one in my life so I went out to buy a book about the labyrinth motif and its impact on spiritual growth. I saw that they came in all shapes and sizes and that people built them for their own private use. I have a good size field just beyond my front yard and it has always had a special feel because of the presence of a huge old oak tree that shaded the area. It was the perfect place for a labyrinth because it already felt sacred. But before I could enlist my husband in such a project I knew we had to walk one.

"We found a private labyrinth on the coast near Monterey and took the weekend to go check it out. What a great labyrinth it was! Built of sand mounds and flowers, complete with dream catchers and gazing balls. I loved it instantly and it confirmed my belief that we could and should have one on our property. I also realized it didn't have to be perfectly flat or perfectly laid.

"Almost immediately my husband and I started gathering stones and rocks on all our journeys. We had a shared vision. We live in the Sierra foothills and knew we could make it of rock from the high country and stones from the rivers and it would cost little or nothing. We gathered them on woodcutting days and had rock-gathering picnics. It is not uncommon for us to pull off the highway at the sight of a great rock that calls out to us. This labyrinth has a lot of granite and crystal, which gives it a powerful energy. It also includes rocks that friends and acquaintances have brought us from all over the world, including Loch Ness, Scotland. Within six months we had enough stones and rocks to lay a good-sized Cretan labyrinth.

"We sat down in the area where we wanted it to be and decided that we wanted the sun at our backs when we entered in the morning and the sun setting behind our beautiful old oak tree in the evening. I made a hand labyrinth out of clay to get the feel of the layout before we actually put it in the yard. My husband, youngest daughter, Jillian, her boyfriend, and I laid it out in about three hours.

"It's pretty big because we had to include enough space in the path for a lawn mower to get through. I asked for a small Weedeater for Mothers' Day so I could help with the upkeep in the spring when the grasses get waist high. It is a living entity.

"I can't stress enough how much having the labyrinth here has changed the feel of our home. Everyone is nicer. We can see it from every room in the house except the bathroom and back bedroom. We see it when we drive away and it is there to welcome us when we come home. It has given us a focus and continual reminder of the spiritual journey we are all on.

"But it is much more than that. It is joyful! Tending it is a form of prayer. Watching it change with the seasons gives us an opportunity to reflect on and connect to the cycles of seasons and the cycles of life itself. I've walked it and run it and some day I might even crawl it. It is always accepting of me, of all of us. All our cats and Zoe my dog follow me down in the mornings and play among the stones while I do my daily walk. It is an event. My three-year-old grandson helps straighten the stones as he checks for worms and can almost make the whole journey in without finding something else more interesting that captures his attention. Jillian sometimes sleeps in its center and says that it is teaching her the importance of dedicating time to her spirit by going within.

"Right now, with the need for peace and brotherhood in the world the center holds a world globe as continual prayer for all of us. I hope some day to have workshops and community rituals … and we're still gathering stones."

Landscape Art

Growing up on the west coast of Ireland, where his playground was the beaches, rock pools, and heather-clad hills of County Donegal, Jim Buchanan became involved with nature's raw elements from an early age. Today, he describes himself as a land artist, someone for whom the natural environment is his canvas, the land providing him with a rich and varied palette of materials and colors.

Jim has undertaken numerous environmental art projects in the UK and abroad, including those for the Writtle College of Horticulture in Essex, at Tapton Park for Chesterfield Borough Council and at Sweetheart Abbey for the Dumfries and Galloway Council Access Arts Program. Jim has a way of walking the equivalent of the Cretan labyrinth in certain cities – the only pre-requisite being the ability to move!

"When I was a child I used to love exploring the ancient burial cairns and standing stones of pre-Christian times and I think it's from this that I developed so much inspiration and experienced so much excitement from the enigmatic structures of the Donegal landscape where I grew up.

"Both my parents are talented ceramic artists and used the labyrinth design in their work; they made labyrinth pendants in the 1970s so I was exposed to this pattern by them. The

local beaches became my drawing board, where I would mark out a labyrinth and watch with a child's pleasure as the sea reclaimed my work.

"In my role as a land artist, I adapt and create labyrinthine forms. I'm less concerned with artistic originality, more with producing something that is sympathetic to that place, inspiring to visit and in harmony with the particular ecology. For instance, in Europos Parkas Sculpture Park in Vilnius, Lithuania (featuring over 70 exhibits in natural settings by artists from all over the world) I created a delicate labyrinth by re-arranging vast quantities of forest materials by hand. Although the humidity of the forest causes everything to decompose very quickly, if only a small percentage of the park's annual 40,000 visitors walk my labyrinth then a new labyrinth will be created from their steps.

"I continue to be intrigued by the way we perceive labyrinths of all scales – from a small design sketched on the back of an envelope through to monumental designs where it's impossible to see what you are walking through. A lot of special energies are associated with labyrinths and I do believe that this pattern has an inherent energy – just as drawing a circle in the sand will have an effect. Few of us spend enough time in meditative contemplation, myself included, and it seems only when we structure our time to visit and walk a labyrinth that we feel able to truly calm down.

"But this experience is available to us pretty much anywhere. Despite being a country boy at heart, I see cities as being labyrinthine in nature and concept, so it seemed natural to me *to develop them as circular routes. Each city, like different labyrinth designs, compels me to walk it in a different way. In Amsterdam I have walked a labyrinthine route twice. This is an interesting city with a series of semi-circular routes and canals that have a resonance with the Cretan labyrinth. It is a fun route and I've felt refreshed by both journeys.*

"Glasgow, however, is very square and has a harder, faster feel, which doesn't leave me rested by the experience. However, I think this is an interesting concept to develop — the city as labyrinth — and I have made sketch plans for routes in Edinburgh, Stuttgart, London, Zurich, and beyond."

Sometimes it happens that an otherwise ordinary event sparks off a passion that changes your life forever. This was certainly the case for Kathy Doore.

The Hero's Journey

Kathy received a postcard depicting the ancient Andean sanctuary of Machu Picchu in Peru, but it took her 12 years to get there as she was struggling to grow her business at that time. Eventually, she was rewarded with a trip in 1990 — after which things would never be the same again.

"A series of odd synchronicities surrounding my receipt of a photo postcard originally beckoned me to Machu Picchu, 'the lost city of the Incas.' Little did I know that my life as I knew it would be forever changed by this seemingly inconsequential event. When I first traveled to Peru, life in that part of the world was not peaceful and quiet, like it is now. As I was deciding whether or not to go, I picked up the magazine section of my local Sunday newspaper with its unusual black cover on which was written four words in red: 'To Die in Peru.' The cover story detailed the events of two recent tourist attacks that had taken place near the Inca Trail.

"Everyone was concerned about me and tried to persuade me not to visit, but I just knew that I had to honor an inner commitment that had found its time of fulfillment. I thought about my options and weighed them carefully, and then determined that even if I must face a physical death in order to find my spiritual life, I was willing to make that commitment. I did not want to continue living my life as I had. My inner knowing told me that this was my moment of transformation, that I had better not miss it.

"While I didn't suffer a physical death in Peru, I did experience a spiritual one. That night, in the ancient sanctuary of the Incas as I sat on an altar stone praying in one of the temples of Machu Picchu, a bolt of electricity shot up through my spine and out the top of my head. Stunned, I was later to learn that I had experienced the rising of the Kundalini – a rare, but natural phenomena that would turn my world upside down (see page 16). When the Kundalini rises one is catapulted into a terrain of deep manifestation, and psychic gifts. The Kundalini is the mythical serpent goddess said to rise through the chakras piercing each in turn, as the human soul journeys towards enlightenment. Less then 48 hours later I found myself in the Amazon rain forest where I contracted dengue fever and by this time, feverish and weak, had to be airlifted out of Peru. I was very ill for weeks but as I emerged from this initial metamorphosis, much of my old life began to fall away, making way for the new. I rediscovered latent abilities, including the sensing of energy fields, and, this I learned had a name, 'dowsing.'

"In 1994 I attended my first dowsers convention hosted by the American Society of Dowsers in Vermont. It was here that I was first introduced to the labyrinth. This was a temporary construction of oddly arrayed survey stakes and colorful plastic tape placed on the lawn of the college campus housing the event. I didn't know what to make of this strange contraption but once everyone had gone to bed, I ventured outside and sheepishly entered it.

"As I began to make my way through the winding pathways I became suddenly aware of shifting energy fields throughout my body. When I exited the labyrinth, I knew I had found an important key to my path and went about learning as much as possible about this ancient tool known for transformation. The first thing I did was to build one on a friend's property, subsequently receiving several commissions to install labyrinths in other locations, including South America.

"On one occasion I had just completed a labyrinth for a couple who had purchased land in the Sacred Valley of the Incas, near Cusco, Peru, on which they planned to build a healing sanctuary. The day we were to return home, I had a dream urging me to backtrack to a nearby resort to ask the owners if they were interested in having a labyrinth built for them. I acted on my intuition and ended up building two Cretan-style turf labyrinths for the Incaland Hotel in Urubamba. I am told the labyrinths have become very popular and are being walked by thousands of spiritual pilgrims on their way to Machu Picchu.

"The labyrinth has served as a metaphor for my own life's path. I was an ordinary woman who was destined to take a different path – the soul's path – during which I was charged with facing my own worst fears. After a period of withdrawal I knew that what was important was to take my gifts back to the outside world where I now teach, write and assist other people in their own spiritual quest.

"Life is all about being open to change and willingly going where the path leads you. As the years have gone by, I've become more involved in organizing an annual pilgrimage to the ancient Andean goddess sites of Peru, including Machu Picchu, as well as introducing people to the Incan temples, one of which is called Q'enqo, a Quecha term meaning 'labyrinth.'"

A New Career

Jeff Saward was first ensnared by labyrinths while attending an astronomy conference in Winchester in 1976 where he encountered the Mizmaze that is cut into the turf on the summit of St. Catherine's Hill overlooking the city. From that moment, Jeff was overcome with a host of questions – who, why, when? – that nobody at the City museum or tourist information office could answer.

"Intrigued by the origin and purpose of the Mizmaze I searched my college library for answers. Finding a copy of W.H. Matthews' 1922 classic study launched my mission to visit other turf mazes that I discovered were scattered across the English countryside. Over the next couple of years I gradually accumulated enough information from my visits and discussions with the owners of these mysterious monuments to produce a booklet that included plans of the labyrinths and maps that could help others find them. Two hundred copies of the first edition sold fast and found their way into the hands of other enthusiasts

who had more information to share with me. So I started a newsletter to keep those folks in contact with each other and, 22 years on, it has grown into the journal Caerdroia *(see Resources). Working with its various contributors over the years has forged firm friendships with fellow researchers, and provided me with many opportunities to visit labyrinths in other countries.*

"Combining my interest in labyrinths with a career in industrial chemistry often meant taking holidays in locations where there were labyrinths to be found. Over the years I've traveled widely, with memorable trips around the Mediterranean islands of Crete, Cyprus and Sardinia, the churches and cathedrals of France, the south-western states of the USA, throughout Scandinavia and the former East Germany. The resulting collection of photographs, guidebooks, and pamphlets soon became a useful resource for other travelers looking for labyrinths. Coupled with my ever-expanding archive of books, papers and magazine clippings, I've increasingly been asked to contribute to publications, videos, and television programs. Each of these projects provides new contacts, opportunities, and learning to keep my interest alive.

"While all of this has been happening in my life, a phenomenal revival of interest in labyrinths has also taken off. Recently, I have been traveling even more frequently to lecture on the history of labyrinths to groups in the USA and Europe. I now work full-time in this capacity with my partner Kimberley Lowelle. Each assignment tends to unearth new labyrinths that we've not seen before and so our collection of photographs continues to grow.

"Although considered by archaeologists and historians as a difficult subject for serious study, labyrinths in their various forms have now gained a new recognition as it's been my good fortune to be invited to participate in a number of research projects. More recently, this has taken me to Arctic Russia in search of the stone labyrinths situated on the shorelines and islands of this remote region.

"A quarter of a century on, while I've managed to answer many of the simple questions I had asked regarding the turf labyrinth at Winchester, each new discovery poses further questions calling for research."

Finally, using the labyrinth symbol played a part in helping many people make sense of the terrorist attack on the World Trade Center on 11 September 2001. Lynne A. Texter, Ph.D., is Associate Professor of Communication at Philadelphia's La Salle University.

Dealing with Grief

La Salle is a private, Roman Catholic University named after John Baptist de la Salle (1651–1719), a former Canon at Rheims Cathedral in France who founded the Christian Brothers schools and was proclaimed Patron of Christian Teachers in 1950. At the University, students are supported in developing worthy personal, social, and religious values. Lynne's story speaks for itself. She entitled it "Roll Out the Rug."

"*We were all stunned. We felt a desperate need to express the fear, the anger, the uncertainty, and the unspeakable sorrow that followed the events of September 11, 2001. We didn't know what to think or what to do, but we knew that we needed to honor the many who had lost their lives and to honor our own intense feelings about all that had happened.*

"*Physically and emotionally close to the brutal attacks, we all seemed to know someone who was or who might have been there: a sister who worked in the World Trade Towers, a friend who was flying out of Boston, a parent who worked at the Pentagon, a neighbor who was visiting New York, an acquaintance who is a New York City police officer, and a former classmate who lives in New York.*

"*When I called to touch base with my father, who intuitively grasped the importance of ritual if not the appropriate language, he asked, 'Are you going to roll out that rug of yours?' That 'rug,' of course, is my 36ft Chartres-style canvas labyrinth, and I have often 'rolled it out' for workshops, presentations, and open walks in times of reflection, bereavement, and celebration. My father's question about opening the labyrinth reiterated that we need not grasp the specifics of the labyrinth to appreciate its power and its role in times when we require a safe and sacred place that can hold whatever people will bring to it.*

"In the days following the September 11th tragedies, including the National Day of Prayer and Remembrance, my colleague and I opened our labyrinth and made it available to our university community in Philadelphia. We are well acquainted with the possibilities of the labyrinth, and we knew it could create a place for everyone to come together. We also hoped that the labyrinth would provide a container for some of the powerful feelings and reactions that so many members of our community were experiencing.

"And so we rolled out the labyrinth and we walked. We walked for those who were lost and for those who were left. We walked the labyrinth and prayed for peace and tranquility, seeking comfort and calm in the aftermath. We walked in search of answers to try to make sense of the senseless acts.

"We walked and walked, and as we did so, the labyrinth brought our many individual journeys together as one. There was a measure of comfort and connection as the community shared the path. Walking with each other to honor, to remember, to celebrate, and to grieve brought the campus community together as never before.

"People visited our labyrinth, singly and together, with friends, with colleagues, with classmates and with those they didn't really know. The bereaved, the sad, the scared, the stunned, and the merely curious gathered together around the Labyrinth as people have for thousands of years.

"The labyrinth has long been a destination for pilgrims of many traditions and with varied intentions. On a pilgrimage, we can see things, sometimes the same things, with new insight. On the face of it, our lives remain unchanged, but beyond the surface, so many things are changed by the journey.

"I have facilitated numerous labyrinth walks and I have walked the labyrinth countless times. But I will long remember the labyrinth walks on the National Day of Prayer and Remembrance. As I witnessed hundreds of people taking this beautiful and age-old pilgrimage to the center and back, I sensed the potential for individual and community transformation. I became aware how deeply we were affected by the events and how much our view of our world had changed. Our lives are not really all that different, but now we are looking at life quite differently as a result of our experience.

"When the day was done, we carefully folded up the Labyrinth. The canvas seemed heavier now, laden with the emotion and heartache of each person who had walked. Ready to be rolled out again, the simple yet profound 'rug' continues to offer a ritual space for all to walk and witness a path of hope and healing."

MAKING A DIFFERENCE

We all have a responsibility to ensure our attitudes and behavior are the most inspiring and honorable that they can be – that we reawaken to the importance of being "of good character" which was once the foundation of all relationships, whether business, social or personal. Maybe the labyrinth is a tool that can help us realize the best, happiest, most fulfilled people we can be. And through that example, you will be a living inspiration to others.

I would love to see labyrinths featured in every school, community center, university, prison, workplace, and public park across the world. Not just to help people find a place of relaxation where they can calm their bodies and minds, but as a constant reminder. As an Islamic sage once said: "Self-knowledge is the shortest road to the knowledge of God." For that to become a reality, each one of us has to take an active role in bringing it about – by helping to build community labyrinths, introducing them into our own homes and gardens and talking about the real-life examples that you have seen or read about.

There are so many ways that you can incorporate labyrinths into your life – from the smallest examples, such as pebbles placed in the form of a three-circuit labyrinth within a flower box, to those that occupy a large section of a field, as with Dr. Alex Champion's earthworks or the animal sanctuary built on Joyce Leake's 60-acre property. You have the option of choosing the number of circuits your labyrinth can have, the style of the design (Cretan, Chartres, or Roman mosaic), the color scheme, the materials you use, whether it is permanent or temporary, and whether you might use it in conjunction with spiritual approaches such as chakra work. It can offer you a compelling approach to meditation, a canvas upon which to explore your creativity and a source of energy with which to balance and harmonize the *chi* that, according to Eastern healing traditions, must flow freely throughout the body.

On top of all this, it is a wonderful catalyst for exploring all manner of subjects from ancient history and mythology to dowsing and sacred geometry. As in the examples you have just read about, labyrinths can play a significant part in focusing the mind to help solve life's challenges. The applications are wide and include children, animals, the elderly, and the infirm, celebrating life and honoring the dead. The appeal of labyrinth is universal because it is not aligned with any particular faith and because, in its simplest interpretation, it is a tool for relaxation and self-expression. It is up to each of you to decide how you may bring the labyrinth into your own life and reap the rewards the journey has to offer.

For myself, I have benefited greatly from writing this book, particularly since this took place at a time when my life was changing beyond all recognition, and I have gained important insights into my own life journey. Plus, this book has brought me into contact with such wonderful, inspiring people who have helped to underscore my belief that all of us "ordinary" folks are incredibly spiritual in our own way.

Enjoy the rest of the journey!

RESOURCES

The following is a small selection of the resources that are available about labyrinths and mazes. I have limited them to those that I know and respect for the quality of the information offered, as well as some that I think you will find of special interest. For those of you with access to the Internet, there is plenty more out there – the last search I did for the word "labyrinth" threw up 610,000 items. Happy reading!

BOOKS

The Art of the Maze, Adrian Fisher and Georg Gerster, (Seven Dials, 2000) – Fisher, a well-known British designer of mazes, explains the secret of mazes and labyrinths found all over the world.

Awaken Your Goddess: A Practical Guide to Discovering a Woman's Power, a Woman's Glory, Liz Simpson (Gaia Books, 2000) – An inspiring diversity of goddess archetypes from around the world and how you can use them in your life.

The Book of Chakra Healing, Liz Simpson (Gaia Books, 1999) – A comprehensive guide to the ancient Indian system of chakras.

Finding Fulfilment: Eight Steps to Achieving Your Ultimate Potential, Liz Simpson (Piatkus, 2000)
— Using the eight-step labyrinth process to help you realize your life's potential.

The Hero with a Thousand Faces, Joseph Campbell (Princeton University Press, 1972) – The
master storyteller outlines the heroic challenges each of us must face as we journey through
life. The inspiration for George Lucas' *Star Wars* films.

Labyrinths: Ancient Myths and Modern Uses, Sig Lonegren (Gothic Image Publications, 1991) –
An excellent guide to the ancient and mythic past of labyrinths by an international writer and
speaker on Earth Mysteries.

The Labyrinth in Culture and Society: Pathways to Wisdom, Jacques Attali (North Atlantic Books,
1999 – This French scholar and economic theorist debates the importance of "relearning
labyrinthine thinking" into our everyday lives.

Mazes and Labyrinths: Their History and Development, W.H. Matthews (Dover Publications, 1970)
— Widely recognized as the original, comprehensive guide to these universal symbols across
the centuries.

The Power of Place and Human Environments, James A. Swan (ed.) (Gateway Books, 1993)
— An inspiring collection of essays celebrating humankind's relationship with Mother
Earth.

The Sand Labyrinth: Meditation at Your Fingertips, Dr. Lauren Artress (Journey Editions, Charles
E. Tuttle Co, 2000) – *The Sand Labyrinth* includes a 10-inch square sandbox, two
traditional labyrinth tops that fit over a layer of fine white sand for finger tracing. The
accompanying book contains sections devoted to using the labyrinth for healing, creativity,
discovering your soul assignment, awakening self-knowledge, and honoring your life.

The Tipping Point: How Little Things Can Make a Big Difference, Malcolm Gladwell (Little,
Brown & Co., 2000) – A theory about why major changes in society (ideas, behaviors, messages,
and products) can happen and spread as quickly and unexpectedly as infectious diseases.

Walking the Sacred Path: Rediscovering the Labyrinth as a Spiritual Tool, Dr. Lauren Artress
(Riverhead Books, 1995) – Dr. Artress is the Canon for Special Ministries at San Francisco's
Grace Cathedral and the creator of the Labyrinth Project.

The Way of the Labyrinth: A Powerful Meditation for Everyday Life, Helen Curry (with Foreword
by Jean Houston) (Penguin Compass, 2000) – A brief introduction to labyrinths followed by
practical guidance on how to use and create them, based on the author's experience as a
labyrinth practitioner.

SELECTED WEBSITES

www.labyrinthproject.com – home of the St. Louis Labyrinth Project and site of Master labyrinth
maker and expert, Robert Ferré. There are canvas labyrinths for sale and rent, labyrinth
products and manuals, free labyrinth-making instructions, plus a large number of labyrinth-
related links.

www.labyrinthos.net – Jeff Saward's international maze and labyrinth resources center, with
photo library and archive. Publisher of *Caerdroia, the Journal of Mazes and Labyrinths*,
containing articles, research, and pictures of European labyrinths. Jeff also offers labyrinth
events and organizes tours of labyrinths around the world. The Labyrinthos site includes an
excellent resources page with a list of UK, Scandinavian and US maze and labyrinth
designers, workshop, pilgrimage leaders, and other useful stuff. Plus the Omphalos forum for

news, speculation, and research related to mazes and labyrinths worldwide. Contact details: Labryinthos, 53 Thundersley Grove, Thundersley, Benfleet, Essex SS7 3EB, UK (Tel: 01268 751915, e-mail: jeff@labyrinthos.net).

www.labyrinthsociety.org – The International society for enthusiasts, annual conferences, and labyrinth directory. Their mission is "to serve the global community by providing education, networking and opportunities to experience transformation" using the labyrinth symbol. Contact details: The Labyrinth Society, PO Box 144, New Canaan, CT 06840-0144, USA (Tel: 877-446-4520, e-mail: Labsociety@aol.com).

www.gracecathedral.org/labyrinth/locator/index.shtml – Grace Cathedral's excellent labyrinth indicator, listing contemporary labyrinths – principally throughout the United States but also in some other countries. Contact details: Grace Cathedral, 1100 California Street, San Francisco, CA 94108, USA.

www.srlabyrinthfoundation.com – Lea Goode-Harris's Santa Rosa Labyrinth Foundation site.

www.earthsymbols.com – information about Dr. Alex Champion's earthworks that he has constructed in the San Francisco Bay Area and Mendocino County, USA.

www.labyrinthcompany.com – David Tolzmann's site for custom-designed canvas walking labyrinths and permanent indoor and garden installations, available in a wide variety of designs, colors, and materials. Studios in Baltimore, Maryland and New York.

www.labyrinthina.com – Kathy Doore's site, labyrinth designer for the Urumbamba site in Peru.

www.labyrinthproducts.com – sells wood finger labyrinths and other products, walking labyrinths for rent or sale in the US, labyrinth education and workshops, plus detailed locations of labyrinths in Illinois, US.

www.lessons4living.com/screensaver.htm – free labyrinth screensaver for Windows.

www.lessons4living.com/drawing.htm – how to draw a seven-circuit labyrinth.

www.geomancy.org/labyrinths/.index.html – Sig Lonegren's Mid-Atlantic Geomancy site.

www.mazemaker.com – Adrian Fisher's site.

www.landartist.co.uk – land Artist, Jim Buchanan's site.

www.ashlandweb.com/forum/labyrinth – an excellent online forum for discussions and queries on finding labyrinth resources.

http://fllc.smu.edu:16080/latin/labyrinth – Prof. Paula Lemmon's Lenten labyrinth.

Other Interesting Websites

www.begehbare-labyrinthe.de/ – German site with some excellent pictures of labyrinths.

www.labyrinthe.at – another German language site.

www.smartbits.nl/labyrinth – mazes and labyrinths in the Netherlands.

http://dowsers.new-hampshire.net/ – the American Society of Dowsers, founded in 1961 to help people learn about the ancient art of dowsing.

www.canadiandowsers.org/ – the Canadian Society of Dowsers.

www.britishdowsers.org – British Dowsing Society.

INDEX